Still Bleating About the Bush

Central Queensland
U N I V E R S I T Y
P R E S S

Marie Mahood

Marie Mahood

Bleating About the Bush first published in 1981 by
National Farmer, a division of Rural Press.
Back at Sundown first published in 1987 by
National Farmer, a division of Rural Press Ltd.

This combined edition published in 1997 by
Central Queensland University Press
PO Box 1615
Rockhampton, Queensland, 4700

National Library of Australia
Cataloguing-in-Publication entry:

   Mahood, Marie
   Still Bleating about the Bush

   ISBN: 1 875998 43 8

   I. Title.

   A823.3

Designed and typeset by Carlin Yarrow
in Times New Roman and Goudy Medieval.

Printed and bound by
Watson Ferguson and Co, Brisbane

Cover painting by Liz Mahood.
Illustrations by Ragai Wanis and Kim Mahood.

Contents

Foreword

Some of these stories were written during the Beef Depression of the Seventies and published in *Bleating About the Bush* in 1981. Others are reprinted from *Back at Sundown*, published in 1987. I hope that I have chosen the most relevant stories from these books, which are both now out of print. I wish to thank Rural Press for their permission to reprint them in one volume. Some might say that a lot of water has gone under the bridge since I first began bleating but actually it hasn't because we've been drought-declared for the last six years and the bleating might now better be described as a doleful howling. (Especially as the weather buffs have just announced another El Nino event while our district is still in the grip of the last one!)

Every cloud has a silver lining. Now, I don't want to be contrary but silver is no darn good to me or any of the battlers in the bush; the blacker the better and sooner rather than later, we say. However, there is every chance that, even as you are reading these words, I am again bleating, this time about devastating floods. That's the way it goes in the bush.

Marie Mahood
Cattle Camp. June 1997.

ARTS QUEENSLAND

Sponsored by the Queensland Office of Arts and Cultural Development

Life in the Northern Territory

Nancy Nabaldjari had been accustomed to running the house unimpeded by any other woman in her domain.

She regarded my arrival with baby Melissa with suspicious mien and every intention of remaining the boss. Which she did.

She did not shilly-shally around with polite suggestions that it might be advisable if her established routine should continue; she made the situation clear on the first morning at 5 am.

Nancy, along with Joe, believed in an early start to the day. She probably called "Missus" a couple of times, but if she did I didn't hear it; after all, it was still pitch dark.

Then she seized me by the shoulders, hoisted me into a sitting position, and shoved a pint-sized pannikin of black tea into my hand.

"Drinkim quickfella!" she ordered.

I thought I was still back in the hospital with that bulldog matron: I drankim, before I realised that I was now home and (a) nominally the mistress of the establishment and (b) I liked milk and sugar in my tea.

Nancy
reigns
supreme

That episode set the standard for the relationship between mistress and house-help which was to continue for the whole year that I lived at Hooker Creek.

Nancy's one weakness was her devotion to the proper prettyfella piccaninny, and as long as I kept my place the household ran smoothly.

I was allowed to change the baby's nappy, but always with a beaming black face hovering at my shoulder, and the preliminary instruction to "washim finger, Missus," the mid-way one to "puttim powder, Missus," and the final one to "gibbit Nancy, Missus." I got to bath the baby on Sundays, when Nancy had a day off, though, as often as not, she appeared to check whether I was doing it properly. She considered Melissa's basket was "whitefella rubbish", and carved her a beautiful wooden coolamon, in which she took her for a walk every afternoon. Is it any wonder that Melissa's first recognisable word was a clearly-enunciated "Nan-seee!"

Nancy's strict household routine was quickly adapted to incorporate Melissa, and of necessity, me.

I made only two attempts to assert my independence. I knew I wasn't going to win over the morning tea at five o'clock, but I did try with rearranging the stores on the pantry shelf one Sunday afternoon.

At six o'clock on Monday morning there was such a racket of banging, thumping, and muttering from the kitchen that I thought it politic to keep out of the way. When I sneaked in later everything in the pantry was back in the place it had been before I interfered.

I pretended I hadn't noticed, and left it that way.

My second revolt was some months later. I was in a snaky mood over something or other, and, without thinking, I took it out on Nancy.

The dear old thing had noticed I was depressed, and had decided to make me a cup of tea, (milk and sugar by now) which she brought to me on a tray with a freshly ironed d'oyley under the teapot, sugar bowl, milk jug, and cup and saucer.

I picked up the cup, inspected it, and said sourly, "There's a tea-stain in the bottom of this cup, Nancy. Take it back to the kitchen and wash it properly, please!"

I don't blame her reaction. She looked at me, took off her apron, slammed it down on the table, and gave notice.

"Me can't work longa too much growlin' bugger; me finish!" and out she stormed.

I was still cranky, so I washed the cup myself, drank my tea, and decided I'd get another house-girl. But Nancy had other ideas.

From mid-morning until sundown she sat cross-legged outside the garden gate, with a red handkerchief tied round her head, and a nulla-nulla across her lap. There were no other applicants for the job. Melissa bawled all the afternoon, and I couldn't find a thing in the pantry.

At five next morning my steaming cup of tea was on the bedside table, and Nancy greeted me with "Morning Missus, proper good day." It WAS a proper good day. I behaved myself after that.

Once Nancy had established that any big ideas I might have had had been dealt with satisfactorily, and that she remained undisputed queen of the kitchen realm, she lowered her defences, and included me in her circle of friends.

A quick cup of coffee in the kitchen after the breakfast washing up, and "Want to hearim good yarn, Missus?" resulted in me being sworn to secrecy and then gleaning all the most scurrilous gossip from the camp, and in a society where plural wives were the norm — one warrior had six wives — the permutations and combinations of extra-marital associations were multiple, fascinating, and sometimes screamingly funny.

Nancy wore the same size pants in her own home as she did in mine.

Her husband, premier tribal rain-maker, was known as Billy-poor-bugger, and

although he had a second younger wife by tribal decree, Nancy, fat and forty, made sure that none of the usual marital plums fell in his lap.

Attractive young Maggie shared the board, and did most of the chores, while an enterprising Nancy arranged her extra-marital contacts and made plausible excuses for her absences.

Billy had once demurred and broken Nancy's arm in a domestic upheaval, but in the end the tongue was mightier than the nulla-nulla, and he, like me, meekly capitulated.

Despite our burgeoning friendship, Nancy had very firm ideas on the strict adherence to correct formal procedures.

In the kitchen we gossiped as equals, but in the dining room, and before visitors, she was the perfect waitress, silent and unobtrusive, serving from the left and clearing from the right, and equally determined that her protégé should be the perfect Missus.

We 'dressed for dinner', usually only Joe and myself at the table. Nancy saw to that, with a freshly-ironed frock laid out on my bed with Joe's long whites at precisely five o'clock each afternoon. SHE chose what I wore.

She did not approve of women in pants, and under no circumstances would she tolerate them if visitors were on the horizon.

When I first appeared in slacks she performed: "Chuckim trouser, Missus! Trouser belong Maluka! Puttim dress allasame proper lady!"

The mailplane called fortnightly, and pilot and passengers had smoko with us in the dining room.

Nancy had no intention of allowing the Missus to let down the side. Every second Saturday every pair of jeans and slacks I owned disappeared from my bedroom, and a dress was presented for wear. I never did find out where she hid my pants.

I believe Nancy was quite proud of me in the end. I had learned that a proper lady did not puttim trouser, talkim loudfella, smokim cigarette, or too much eatim beer — at least in front of 'company'.

When I decided to visit my sister in Darwin, Nancy was torn between the conflicting demands of a properly-run household and the prospect of the pretty-fella piccaninny in incompetent hands. Melissa won, and she came with me.

Naturally Nancy wanted to indulge in the female delights of the Chinese dress-shop, so I accompanied her and she purchased two bright dresses for herself. I shall never forget the look on the shop-assistant's face when Nancy peeled another couple of notes off her roll, slapped them on the counter, and brusquely ordered the assistant to "gibbit dress longa Missus."

Nancy was entranced by my beautiful blonde sister, and when we returned home she sang her praises to Joe to such an extent that Joe told her he was considering taking my sister for a second wife as she was the right tribal skin for him.

That was a different kettle of fish. Nancy's brows drew down and she stamped out to the kitchen to plan a strategy on my behalf.

The upshot was that I was invited to a women's corroboree, organised by Nancy, to "singim-up nother man" for me, to make the Maluka jealous so he might realise that what was sauce for the gander might also apply to the goose.

It was quite a ceremony, taboo to all men, and the uncanny result was that, two days later, we were unexpectedly visited by two young men, and the taller, handsomer one (Nancy had specified handsome) appeared to be taken in by my charms to a degree that was almost embarrassing.

Nancy carried in the tea-tray with a broad smirk, almost, but not quite, gave me a dig in the ribs, and sauntered back to the kitchen with the knowledge of a job well done.

It was well done too, because the fellow in question stayed some days to attend a muster, and it wasn't until Joe mentioned to Nancy that my sister's husband wouldn't agree to sell her, that she agreed to help me evade the advances of the "nother man".

When Melissa graduated from the coolamon to a stroller, Nancy conferred on her the Dreaming of Binta-binta, the butterfly, which would have belonged to her own girl-children if she had had any.

At about the same time, on a visit to a neighbouring station, Nancy introduced me to her mother and brother, not as the missus, or "mother belong piccaninny", but as "friend belong me," and I knew it was one of the greatest compliments I had ever been given.

When we were transferred from Hooker Creek I bawled unashamedly at parting from Nancy, and she did too.

The short time of our acquaintance was an idyllic year, and I realise now, as I did not then, how great a part Nancy played in making it so.

Confessions
from a
country
kitchen

Back in the olden days the first priority of a marriageable female was to be proficient in the culinary arts.

She could be as plain as a pikestaff and have a tongue like a viper, but if she could cook well her position in the family was assured, and her idiosyncrasies tolerated.

What has been overlooked, of course, is that she didn't have a tongue like a viper at the outset of her culinary career.

She was a sweet, biddable female, unfortunately susceptible to the pressures of a society that ordained that her place in life was in the kitchen. It was the cooking that changed her.

It's a bit different in the bush: there are as many, or more, male cooks in the rugged outback as there are females, and everyone knows the saying — 'It's not madmen who take on cooking; it's the cooking sends men mad.'

Many station cooks have found a simple antidote to insidious insanity. Every six months or so they go on a rip-roaring bender for a couple of weeks, and then, revitalised, return to concoct mouth-watering masterpieces for another limited span.

It is not a good idea to disparage or circumvent the benders, for a thwarted cook, already in the first stages of trauma culinatis, may react violently. (Remember the poem 'That Day At Boiling Downs!!'). Contrary to general supposition, they rarely put strychnine in your stew; they usually go berserk with the axe.

When I was a new bride en route to my first home in the bush, we pulled up about sundown at a droving camp.

"Pity yer ain't goin' TO town, insteada comin' FROM," said the drover. "I wanta lift for me cook. His hide's crackin', and he won't cook. So I can't offer yer much of a feed."

I followed his glance to where, twenty yards away, the cook was mumbling to himself, trudging around in circles, one hand swatting at imaginary flies and the other dragging the axe in the dust behind him.

"What's he got the axe for?" I enquired anxiously.

"Dunno," said the drover, "he might be gunna chop some wood, but I ain't sure."

I was glad we were coming from town and not going to; it was three hundred miles to the nearest shanty, and I didn't reckon that cook was going to last the distance.

Females, being conditioned from infancy to the expectation of an adult life slaving over a hot stove, generally react differently.

Gradually, the sunny nature sours, the cranky comments increase, and by middle age the perfect roast dinner is garnished, perforce, with vituperative comment along with the horse-radish sauce, — but seldom does she take to the axe.

For those of you acquainted with the TV series `Prisoner' it is quite obvious that a miscarriage of justice has been perpetrated on Lizzie, sentenced to life imprisonment for merely poisoning the whole shearing team. It was, naturally a case of occupational circumstances, and should have been treated as such.

A female subterfuge to avoid looking at the subject in its true perspective, is to pretend that it is an art-form, and to achieve a certain status as a creator of a special pavlova, or a unique flavour to the pickled onions, or a perfect rice-pudding.

I knew one woman who used to put two eggs and a dollop of honey in her bread dough, and insist to MY menfolk that the trick was all in the kneading. Hypocrite!

My only claim to being creative was to change the name when I burnt the custard. I usually burnt the custard. But one day I didn't have time to make a second lot, so I served it up as 'caramel souffle'. It worked for a few weeks, then, one supper-time, four little kids, seated on a long form behind the table, took up their spoons and beat on the table, chanting in unison, "We hate caramel souffle! We hate caramel souffle!" So I gave it away after that, and made jelly. I can cope with jelly.

You've all seen those ads in the country papers for cooks. There's always that nasty little phrase — must be good bread cook. Bread is the thing you stand or fall by in the bush. There are some people who are born beautiful; there are some who are born talented; and there are some who are born bread-cooks.

And there's me!

The word bread has a nightmare connotation to me. My first effort, when I was young and keen to please, and still an unconscious victim of conditioned reflex, resulted in two horrible little heavy khaki-coloured slabs about four inches high which fell from the tins on to the table with ominous thuds. Joe comforted me with the comment that the yeast must have been too old. He got a new tin of yeast from the store and mixed a new batch, kneaded the dough, put the right sort of wood in the stove, and produced a couple of tall, fluffy-textured loaves that smelt heavenly, and tasted so good that we ate them almost immediately.

Two days later I tried again, so confident that I doubled the flour to make four loaves. Four horrible little heavy khaki-coloured slabs about four inches high fell from the tins on to the table with ominous thuds.

Okay, so I tried putting eggs and honey in the dough: I tried every known variety of yeast: I tried fool-proof recipes given me by half the station cooks in Australia.

I didn't solve the problem until I found out by accident that I could make bread rolls — same dough, same yeast, but twelve rolls instead of one loaf. I wonder whether the trick's in the kneading?

The male cooks have a very low standing on the social scale too. Just look at some of the nicknames they have to put up with in the stock-camp.

"Who's your poisoner this year?"

"Oh, we've got Blue-Bob-the-Bastard-from-Boorooloola. Who's yours?"

"Busted-Oven."

"Had him last year. Cooks a better feed than old Turd-Strangler, but he's not as good as Fourteen-Sods-In-A-Row. "

I know some even worse nicknames, and I guess you do too, but I don't think I could print them.

Cooking's a difficult job, not only because everybody takes you for granted, but because if your loading only comes twice a year you are always likely to run out of necessary ingredients. Bush cooks are expected to be inventive, and they frequently have to produce a meal at a minute's notice for anything up to five or six unexpected visitors.

If you've recently got a killer, it's no worry, because everybody will eat steak, eggs, and onions three times a day. But if you're down to the knuckle and the round you only have three alternatives. You have meat, and you have plenty of vegetables in the station garden, so:

(a) Chop it all up together and boil it. That's stew, but it's not really popular.

(b) Chop it all up, leave out the potato, add curry powder, and serve it with rice. That's curry.

(c) Chop it all up, fry the meat first in peanut oil, add water and vegetables, and serve it with rice. That's Ying Tong Foo.

Actually, if you've got any of (a) left over, you can turn it into (b) by stirring in some curry powder, or (c) by pouring soy sauce all over it. Sounds awful, doesn't it. I pass on my secret for what it is worth.

Somehow I've worked myself into the mood for confessions. There was the time I tried to make sausages. We acquired a mincing machine with a spout on one end to which you attached the sausage-casing. It was fun feeding meat, onions and spices in one end, and watching the writhing, bulging casing twitching and filling at the other end.

I got over-enthusiastic, I suppose. With twenty-two feet of continuous sausage fattening like a voracious boa-constrictor all over the kitchen table, how was I to know the exact moment to stop before it burst and splattered sausage-insides all over table, floor, walls and ceiling?

Making soap wasn't any better. Nobody told me you couldn't add caustic to an aluminium container of bubbling fat. The aftermath was more satisfactory, though, because when the smoke and fumes cleared, the kitchen walls and ceiling were as clean as if they'd been newly painted.

Joe loves sponge cake. Fruit cake leaves him unmoved; chocolate cake, he can take or leave; but on sponge cake he waxes lyrical.

It was his birthday. I got up very early and I made a sponge cake. I followed the directions in the recipe book exactly, and I popped it in the oven, expectantly relishing the pleasure my action would bring. The oven was exactly right — I know it was. Why, then, did I produce a one-inch high sponge cake? I was still staring at it in consternation when Joe came yawning into the kitchen.

"Gee, honey," he said, "you've been cooking early. What a lovely big fat pancake! Just what I fancy for breakfast!" So I squeezed lemon on it, and poured

cream over it, and he ate his birthday sponge, under the impression that it was an odd-tasting pancake.

And there was the time — oh, Lord, I've done it again! Before I sat down at the end of the kitchen table with my typewriter, I plucked and cleaned the chook, I made the stuffing, and I lit the fire. I thought I'd type a page or so while the oven was getting hot. And I've just looked up, and there's a raw chook staring at me from the end of the table. And the fire's gone out! And it's nearly six o'clock!

In moments of stress I turn to doggerel:

"If you have to cook 21 meals and 14 smokos

Every week every year ad infinitum,

When people stick heads in the door,

You've got every excuse to bitum."

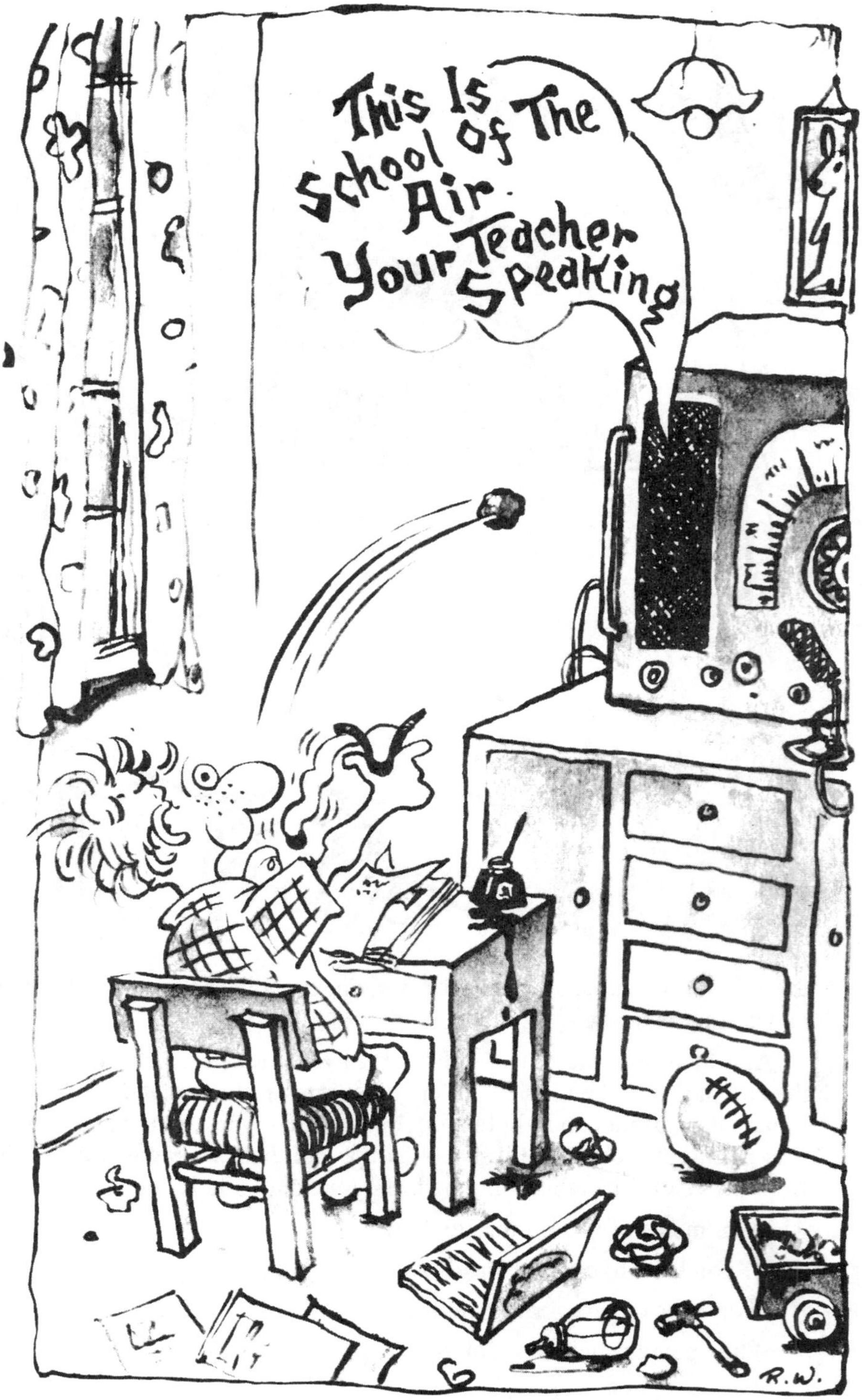

How many feet in a yard?

How many feet in a yard?

You know that education comes first — and I know that education comes first — but try telling that to the kids. (And on occasions when Dad is short-handed he's not much help either.)

It's simple enough to enrol the children at the correspondence school, and if you live in an area where the Wet Season is likely to interrupt your mail service the correspondence school will always send you advance lessons if you ask for them.

The next step is to find a governess, and that can be a ticklish one.

If you find a good one, hang on to her at all costs. Give her bonuses; if she likes riding, give her a horse; some mothers of large families have even been known to marry her off to an eldest son just to keep her on the property.

Perhaps your governess turns out to have a wonderful personality, but she's shaky on the spelling, and her mathematical ability is limited by the number of her toes and fingers; trade jobs with her — she probably loves cooking and housework, and there's your chance to learn the metric system properly, and you can convince Dad you're not just a pretty face, by converting gallons of dip into litres quicker than he can.

Having solved the problems of lessons and supervisor, we come to the major factor — depriving the kids of their liberty for an average of five hours each week-day, and making them work.

Don't take any notice of the education experts, or Doctor Spock, or the Women's Weekly — they've never had to deal with station kids incarcerated in the school-room while the stockmen are trying out the new colts down in the homestead yards, or the farm kids who can hear the enraged bellows of their father abusing the new farmhand who's just driven the tractor over — well, not quite over — the septic-system pit.

There's only one tried and true method of making farm kids do their schoolwork amicably. Bribery.

If you don't like the connotations of that word, you can call it the same as the political parties and the smart businessmen do — it's an Incentive System. It

"Every time you get one week ahead with your schoolwork, Johnny, you can go out with the stock-camp for a week. "

"You can have a new saddle, Mary Anne, just as soon as you get ten merit cards for your schoolwork. "You get the idea? You need to do a bit of planning. Don't be talked into this flexi-time racket. Set a time to begin lessons, a definite smoko time and lunch hour, and so on, and don't deviate from it unless the bushfire has reached the house yard or the floodwaters are lapping the verandah. In that case, declare a holiday and make them work Saturday.

It's possible that you may have a little misunderstanding now and then with the teachers who correct the lessons, but you can explain to an indignant child that teachers are human beings just like the rest of us, so they can make mistakes too.

It's not easy to placate a five-year-old who has failed a comprehension reading test — DRAW A DRUM — when she knows perfectly well that she drew a forty-four — I mean a 200 litre-drum, but it can be done. When she calms down, you can tell her about the other sort of drum.

And at least you don't have to contend nowadays with the six-year-old who answers the question: "How many feet in the yard?" with the comment "depends on how many cattle in it!"

For outback children School of the Air is of enormous benefit, not only as a help with the actual lessons, but because the children are members of a class, and for a set time each day they can talk to each other and their teacher.

They may only meet once a year at the School of the Air get-together, but they can join in singing lessons, class plays, and Christmas concerts, which would not otherwise be possible.

For families which do not normally have a transceiver the Education Department will allocate one for school use only, equipped with a special channel for School of the Air.

The once-a-month Mothers' Meeting on this channel is the equivalent of a normal school's Parents' and Friends' Association.

Being asked questions you can't answer is something we all come up against, and the best way around this is an encyclopedia, not the expensive kind, but the ones you can buy weekly from the newsagent until you've built up the set. They are really good, because the kids read them each week as they arrive, and they are written so the children can understand them easily.

All things considered, the child on correspondence has a number of advantages over the town child, the main one being that he works at his own pace and covers everything in the lessons, so that he gains a solid understanding of the basics. If he's sick, or misses school for some reason, he picks up where he left off, so he does not miss work essential to future understanding.

If your maths lessons don't insist on learning tables, make the kids do it anyway. (Maybe calculators are widely available, but the batteries have a nasty habit of running down when you're 200 miles from the nearest store.)

As a high-school teacher now, I have noticed that the children who learned their tables by rote are coping far better than those who didn't, and high-school maths teachers are currently teaching tables to teenagers in remedial classes.

The same thing can be said for spelling and grammar — they're basic, no matter what the educational theorists say about it. Your own commonsense is far more valid than the verbal diarrhoea from the ivory towers, and you know your child far better than the pontificating psychologist, who frequently labours under the delusion that no child ever has a bout of sheer cussedness for no good reason, and that every child is self-motivated.

You don't turn out a good sheep-dog by waiting for him to become self-motivated, and you don't turn out a good scholar by waiting until little Johnny "feels like" doing lessons. Chances are he'll never feel like it, and if he does, but at irregular times, it's going to play hell with your routine. So no advice from the so-called experts; you're the expert where your child is concerned, and common-sense is the yardstick.

Another big advantage is that the child on correspondence lessons has individual, or almost individual teaching, so you can correct all his mistakes, which is not possible in a normal classroom, and you'll probably get through the set work in less time than the town school-day.

It's a good idea to make Johnny work at a reasonable pace so he forms the habit of working quickly, and thus won't have difficulty in keeping up with the rest of the class when he goes away to high school.

There's a lot written these days about children being "socially-adaptable" and "fitting in with the peer group". Comfort yourself with the knowledge that if your child has some initial difficulty in conforming to the habits of his peers, he's probably far better at fitting into the "family group", which is a lot more important.

But do warn him that when the class teacher looks up from her desk and says "who threw that paper aeroplane?" she does not expect an honest answer, and if Johnny raises his hand and says politely, "Billy Smith did, Miss," he's in for a thumping in the playground.

If Johnny threw the aeroplane himself, and admits to it, his classmates will think he's nuts, and give him a wide berth. If he follows the "when in Rome, do as Rome does" advice he should get by, and if you don't approve of some of his more obnoxious "social-adaptations" you can always knock it out of him in the holidays.

Snips, snails and

puppy dog tails

Snips, snails and
puppy dog tails

I think the School of the Air is a wonderful thing.

But I didn't altogether approve when the School-of-the-Air teacher asked the kids to collect specimens for a nature display in the studio.

I heard the voice of doom and made pathetic flapping movements with my hands. Past experience flashed a warning signal, and I leapt for the switch of the transceiver, but — too late!

Sammy, Frankie, Mandy and little Peter never did anything by halves. Enthusiasm and an insatiable curiosity are two of their more obvious traits, and the request was tailor-made for them.

Sammy said they could start with Mandy's bats; Mandy said no, they could not, and bit him. Mandy's bats were somewhat of a trial to me; I wouldn't have had any real objection if they had started with Mandy's bats.

Black Bat lived in the dining-room under the Queen Anne dining table. He was a vague, diminutive, friendly little bat, given to fluttering around under the table in the shadows, and he was really no trouble except when we had visitors and ate in state in the dining-room.

Mandy used to remove him and hang him up behind the sideboard, but he always managed to get back under the table by the time we sat down.

We had a dowager-type English lady once, who'd managed to give me the impression that she wasn't particularly impressed by barbaric Australian customs. So I'd laid on all the frills to uphold the honour of my native land.

Everything went very well until the dessert.

Then Black Bat decided to take a flutter around our knees. I felt him swish past. The English lady must have felt his passing too, because I saw her glance swiftly at the ringer on his best behaviour seated beside her, and then look puzzled when she registered that both his hands were on the table.

Bat went past again, and Lord know what the old girl was thinking. So I thought I'd better explain it was only Black Bat before she slapped someone's face. Who'd have thought the stupid woman would leap up shrieking, and spill wine all over my best tablecloth!

Brown Bat was an entirely different character. He lived on a saucer on Mandy's dressing-table, and he was an aggressive, demanding little bat, given to interrupting conversations with fierce clashings of sharp little teeth. And nobody could say he fluttered; he zoomed.

In the summer we used to eat at a long table on one end of the verandah, and at some stage during the evening meal you could depend on Brown Bat to emerge from Mandy's bedroom at the other end of the verandah, and hurl himself like a bullet straight down the length of the verandah and straight at the face of one of the family. Two inches from collision point he would change course either right, left, or up. He'd land on a rafter, wait a minute or two, and then launch himself into the charge back. Sometimes he did it three or four times a meal, and it was quite disconcerting until you got used to it.

Mad Bat didn't live in the house, but he always came in at night-time. He flew as if he had the hiccups, and you'd see him in the dusk, making his erratic way towards the lighted verandah, narrowly missing tree branches and clothes-lines.

I don't know why he continued coming, because Brown Bat beat him up a couple of times, and he fluttered and blundered and bumped into things, and was altogether a born loser.

Once he flew into the doorpost and knocked himself out, but Mandy gathered him up, and put water on his brow with an eye-dropper, and he came-to after a few minutes. The fireflies in the rafters scared him stiff; he used to squeak with panic and flop straight down to the floor.

But let us back to the nature display!

Time: 5.30 am. Place: my bed on the verandah. I am dreaming that a herd of bison is thundering down upon me, and the thundering is very lifelike. Too lifelike! I come awake, and spring to a sitting position, and am hit in the eye by an owl. The owl moves on, and four kids and a dog hurdle my bed as they circumnavigate the house in raucous pursuit.

Have you been bitten by a fat-tailed marsupial mouse just put in your tea caddy until they find a better place? Have you bailed forty-seven red-spotted burrowing frogs out of your troughs before you can rinse the washing? Have you found seventeen elephant grubs in your five-year-old's school desk, and the eighteenth squashed in the zipper of his pencil case?

In vain did I plead that live specimens were of no use to the School-of-the-Air display. They'd thought of that. The little darlings had collected all the reasonably-fresh corpses they could find and pickled them in my jam-jars. They had cartons of cocoons and a rat's skeleton; they had ant-lions, and apus, and assorted water-beetles — silver-chested, diving, and giant South-American — in serried ranks of jars and tins lined-up on their dressing-tables, and now, in the interest of science, they had decided to "observe" the living things.

What has science got that I haven't got? I can't get an hour's work out of them without reproachful glances and veiled comments about Lord Shaftesbury. But two eleven-year-old boys, an eight-year-old girl, and a five-year-old boy dug, in two days, a pit six feet by six feet by four feet deep.

"Snakes fall in 'em," said my sweet little daughter with relish. Travellers beware! Don't move an inch off the main road. The Australian equivalent of elephant pits scars the bushland around our homestead.

In a misguided moment we'd allowed some bird and animal natural history books to infiltrate our library, and now — devouring data, dissecting corpses, mangling Latin names, and filling our home with hordes of horrible creatures — the brood has devised a fiendish punishment for that thoughtless act.

Gerald Durrell's mother never had it so good. She only had one. I've got four, and fifteen-year-old Melissa, who comes home in the holidays and directs operations with the precision of a high-class general.

There go the last of my preserving jars, and a third bedroom becomes the haunt of geckos, lizard eggs hatching with the rapidity of machine-gun fire, pet scorpions, and assorted marsupials and their sand-trays.

I accustomed myself to the daily perambulation of a three-foot rough-tail goanna along the verandah rafters; I meekly removed the piebald excreta of an errant gecko from my bedroom mirror; I didn't pull out the plug when the bath was full of apus — I put them in a bucket. I've been bitten, I've been stung, and I've been hit in the eye with an owl.

I've sat up nights with ailing wallabies. Other nights have been rendered sleepless by the keening of a dingo named Melody on the back lawn. I never did find out what transformed Sammy into the lumpiest allergy case ever seen.

Little Pete collected caterpillars. Not just a few — caterpillars by the bucket, caterpillars by the tonne, striped ones, horned ones, great green monsters with fearsome eyes on the rear ends, and a few "special" ones.

And who's the mug who provides provender for the hosts of steadily-chomping caterpillar jaws? You've guessed it! And they ALL have their special leaves. And I fell in an elephant pit when I was getting last night's supply!

I guess I can take it. I guess it isn't really the School-of-the-Air teacher's fault.

He only accelerated what's been going on here for a long time. But I do resent that owl!

(Dear Editer — We have red what our mother rote. Sammy sneaked it and red it to us. She is a good mother but sumtimes she eggzadgerats. It wasent fourty-seven frogs, it was only thirty-seven, and the owl dident realy hit her it only just sort of swooped at her. The poor thing was fritened becos it coudent see proply in the daytime.

Sammy ses if it cood see it would have knowed better than to swoop at Mum, she gets so mad.

And we have realy only got two pits, it got too hard to dig, and we dident catch mutch anyway, only one snake, a marsoopial mouse, three frogs, and Mum. She yelled and got mad.

Sammy ses wheres her sens of hoomer. Frankie thinks we ort to fill them in now in case we catch Dad. Dad hasent got any sens of hoomer either. Pete ses good job if we do but thats becos Dad sat on his speshul caterpilla last night when he just put it down for a minit. Love from Mandy.)

All the gardening books have chapters on pests, and how to deal with them, but none of them ever mention the sort of pests we have. I grew, out in the desert, mind you, the most luscious crop of strawberries imaginable. For a couple of weeks we ate huge red strawberries with our breakfast cereal, and I planned on a pantry shelf laden with pots of strawberry jam.

I used to take my basket about five o'clock every evening to pick the fruit, so I was quite taken aback one day to find very few strawberries and a stuffed blue-tongue lizard lying on its back in the shade of the plants, with front paws clasped over its distended belly, and crimson juice dribbling from its jaws.

Gremlins in the garden

I abused it, and ejected it from the garden, and it waddled off, breathing heavily, and dragging its stomach along the ground.

It was there again next day, same position, same replete expression. I suppose a short, sharp jab with a shovel might have brought the matter to a satisfactory conclusion from my point of view, but it didn't seem quite the right thing to bash a blue-tongue while it lay on its back in euphoric contemplation of the near-by larder.

Bluey and I shared the strawberries, and I only made three pots of jam.

Did you know that cats adore asparagus? Catnip would have been old-hat to our cat, Louie. I used to cut my asparagus spears at about four inches, and they could be eaten as a hot vegetable, as well as cold in salads.

That is, until Louie discovered them. He beat me up every morning, adjourned to the garden, and breakfasted on asparagus tips with purring pleasure. You could tell from his little paw-prints that he'd been jumping up and down with delight, as he nipped off each new shoot.

I didn't share the asparagus with Louie. He got the lot. I was just the mug who kept watering the plot for him.

I was always justly famed for my tomatoes — both in the man world and the bird world! Deep green foliage, great firm red fruit, and in the trees surrounding the garden, a hundred crow-eyes covertly watching the fruit ripening. An absence of a couple of hours from the homestead, and it was "Come on boys! Squadron One take the rockmelons, and First Platoon, direct to the tomatoes!"

I caught a laggard once with a well-aimed rock, and he fluttered squawking to the ground. Thereupon his erstwhile mates attacked him, so I drove them off, and found he had an injured wing. He pleaded for life with such pathetic guttural pleas and promises that what could I do but let him convalesce in the house garden on a diet of chook-feed and house scraps.

We share our present crop of tomatoes with the bower birds. The small plot is close to the kitchen door where the crows don't approach because dogs and cat are in close proximity.

But dogs, cats, and humans are no match for our bower birds. They can imitate anything, and one makes the sound of a dog lapping water, another mews enticingly, while a third chops wood or mutters imprecations, so I know perfectly well that the environs of the kitchen door are a hive of activity.

What I don't know is that there is really not a soul in sight, and there's not a vestige of a tomato bush visible for the load of gorging bower birds silently stuffing while their mates supply the distracting sound effects.

I had a sweetcorn crop once that would have taken a first in any agricultural show — a couple more days, and the cobs were to be harvested. I drooled over them, and mentally buttered and peppered and salted them, and made plans for a six-months supply of deep-frozen corn.

But Mr Nobody left the garden gate open, and I awoke on the morning of corn-harvesting to find eight plump heifers frolicking with tassels of corn-silk dangling from their jaws, and not even a stump of a plant still standing.

I can't eat corn to this day without a vision of a skittish heifer with a great blue-grey tongue snaking out and sweeping the last remnants of corn-silk down to its bovine stomach.

Joe's best stud bull and I had a running feud for twelve months. He fancied grape-vines, passion-fruit vines, and roses. The Aborigines called him Best Bull, but the kids and I called him Bad Bull.

In the open range country there aren't any fences, and in establishing the station, the fencing off of the homestead area was a fair way down on the list of immediate priorities. Kids on horses would muster Bad Bull and escort him twenty miles away to another bore, but some time in the same night a furtive scrunching at the vines ten feet from the verandah would announce his return.

I wanted a pergola of grape-vines to shade the verandah: you could practically say I was obsessed with the need of a pergola of grape-vines. I planted slips daily, and Bad Bull consumed them nightly. The great brute would tippy-toe in and reef them out, chomp them up, and then bellow a challenge as he retreated via the watered area where I was trying to establish a lawn, adding insult to injury as he bogged through the wet grass.

I took to sleeping on the verandah adjacent to the vines, with a .22 and an old school bell handy. The slightest rustle would waken me, and I'd rush out, pyjamaed, into the night, firing shots into the air, ringing the bell wildly, and shouting abuse.

Bad Bull's tally dropped, but the ringers started to complain about broken sleep, and once an unprepared Sydney visitor thought we were being attacked by hostile Aborigines, and spend the rest of the night quivering in abject terror under his bed.

This method, or variations of, is not uniquely mine. Joe recalls approaching a neighbouring station about ten o'clock one night to hear a fusillade of 303 shots and an awe-inspiring cacophony of terrified braying.

He braked as a flurry of furiously galloping donkeys swept across the road in front of him, and behind them his headlights picked up the junoesque form, white-nightie-clad and barefooted, of our neighbour's wife, still blasting away at the retreating herd.

She jumped into the vehicle, rode back to the homestead with him, parked the 303 in the comer of the kitchen, and put the billy on for a cuppa with enquiries after the welfare of our family, and only a bare reference to the depredations of the wild donkeys.

I beat Bad Bull in the end. Mutterings from the staff after one of my bullets went perilously close to the quarters, persuaded Joe to upgrade his priority list and fence in the homestead.

I gleefully examined Bad Bull's tracks each morning as he walked up the outside of the new fence, through the gap, and down the inside to the vines. The gap narrowed daily, but he persevered right to the bitter end.

I supervised the erection of the gate across the road at sundown one evening, and it was balm to my ears as I lay in bed that night and listened to the thwarted bellows of the brute on the OTHER side of the fence.

So much for above-the-ground pests; of the underground ones white ants are the most persistent. The poor plant is attacked above-ground by bulls, cats, crows, bower birds, lizards and grasshoppers, and from below by steadily-chewing white ants. And they don't always keep their places below either.

A fine crop of watermelons was turned into a termite village when they tunnelled up, entered the melons from below, and hollowed out the middles. I noticed small, perfectly-circular holes in the melon rinds one day, knelt down to inspect them further, and came nose-to-nose with a termite, peering out of its window and examining me with a proprietary air. Just about every melon had a white ant twitching its whiskers at the window.

Sometimes you don't get the results the garden books lead you to expect, especially when you have casual garden help.

I'm not having a shot at Aborigines, or at half-wits; it's just coincidence that poor old George was both.

He dearly wanted a job, but he didn't have the courage to ask for it himself, so a big tall Aborigine approached the boss on his behalf. Joe could hear a funny, teeth-grinding noise coming from behind the boy as they conversed: that was George.

Joe didn't actually sight him because every time he stepped sideways George slid to the opposite side of his mentor, but it was finally arranged that George take up duty as garden-boy. Instructions were given, and the Aborigine and a contented grinding noise went off to the camp.

What we didn't know then was that you not only had to tell George what to do, you also had to tell him when to stop doing it.

Shown in the morning how to dig around the first fruit tree and build a circular bank to hold in the water, George was left to it.

About eight o'clock that night two mildly-accusing black boys coughed outside the back door.

"What about George, boss?"

"Well, what about George?" queried Joe.

"`im allabout work, you tellim stop now!"

By torchlight George was revealed still stolidly digging, at the bottom of a pit among the exposed roots of an orange tree, and in a long line behind him the toppled fruit trees bore mute testimony to his day's industry.

After that, we decided to restrict him to watering. I remember him standing with a bag over his shoulders in the middle of a fierce tropical downpour, up to his ankles in running water, but still hosing determinedly.

He never could master the intricacies of pushing the hose through the netting wire so it would reach the surviving fruit trees outside the garden. His instinct for keeping out of sight involved him in manoeuvring so that there was always some obstacle between himself and any other person, and he couldn't concentrate on keeping out of sight and doing his job at the same time. This frequently led him into situations he couldn't handle.

A frantic crescendo of teeth-grinding one day alerted me to the fact that all was not well in the garden.

George had successfully pushed the hose through a hole in the netting and watered the trees. Then, obviously, he wanted the hose back inside the garden, and at this stage the project fell apart.

Instead of pulling the hose back through the same hole, he had pushed the nozzle back inside through a second hole. Something was wrong — the hose was too short. He pushed the nozzle back outside again, this time utilising a third hole. Shorter still!

He ground his teeth perplexedly. He had another try on hole number four, and then he panicked. He threaded that hose in and out of that fence, water still spurting from the nozzle, bleating and grinding frantically, until suddenly there was no more hose left to thread.

I did not dare to approach for fear of un-nerving him altogether, so I called out from a distance — "Okay, George, finish now, smoko time!" and he dropped the nozzle he was trying to tug through the fence, and fled.

I sneaked into the garden, turned off the tap, and unlaced sixty feet of hose. I think the sound around me was the humming of dragonflies, but it may have been me grinding my teeth.

Fowl play: agony and eggstacy

When your nearest store is four hundred-odd miles to the south-east at Alice Springs, it's a good idea to raise your own chooks.

When the homestead consisted of only a bore and a bough shed, where Joe, the contractors, and the black boys camped at irregular intervals, there was always a chance that a little scavenging would provide fresh eggs to vary their dry-rations diet, because neighbourly Gerry had released twenty-two bantams in the environs of the camp soon after it was set up.

You only had to hunt around, find a nest, crack the eggs into a pannikin first to sort out the rotten ones, and there was breakfast.

Later donations of fowls included white leghorns from the Kimberleys, black orpingtons from Alice, and a couple of rhode island reds and a speckly rooster and hen which just materialised.

When the homestead was nearly completed some months later, the children and I left Alice Springs for our new home, and a friend pressed a parting gift on us — six aristocratic white bantams with lovely fluffy trousers right down to their dainty feet.

Joe had vaguely said, "There's chooks there!" But I hadn't really envisaged the colony of wild, self-supporting, egg-concealing birds that inhabited the surrounding mulga.

The men helped us to unload furniture and unpack gear for a few days, and then left us to settle in while they answered the insistent calls of the cattle somewhere out in the sandhills. We completed our initial settling, and then I turned my attention to chooks and garden.

There was the ideal chook-house — a vast bough-shed with thick spinifex roof. All we had to do was clear it out, enclose it with netting wire, and build a strategic gate.

Eight-year-old Sammy appointed himself chook-boy. He built perches and nests, and located two bedourie ovens for water containers. Over two or three days kids and governess rounded up assorted roosters, hens and chickens, and introduced them to a more civilised existence.

When the men returned three weeks later I was in real trouble. I had pinched their bough-shed, their home, their haven of coolness. I had piled their cyclone stretchers, their packbags, and their bush table in the new shed. The new shed, with its cement floor, and the brand-new homestead, were no substitute for their erstwhile home!

A woman and kids introduced into a former all-male society spelt trouble, they knew, but this was altogether too much. There were mutterings about pulling out, and I had to sweet-talk for about six weeks before I gradually wore them down.

Meanwhile I accepted baskets of eggs daily from Sammy and was too busy to give a thought to what was happening down in the bough-shed chookhouse. What was happening was that Sammy was training fighting cocks, and organising bouts for the entertainment of the staff after working hours, with a profitable little bookmaking venture on the side.

Big black Sonny Liston was a popular fighter, but Cassius Clay ran him close. The favourite was probably Lionel Rose, the most aggressive black bantam in the business, who fought any rooster to a standstill, though he be four times his weight and size. The speckly rooster was Chickenheart; he invariably ran away to fight another day.

Mum's trousered bantam cock was excused combat; Sammy always did know where to draw the line.

I was vaguely aware that parts of the bough-shed had been divided off and various hens were sitting on clutches of eggs. My son discoursed glibly on

Mendel's Law, and he spent so much of his time with the chooks that I was ready to believe that he really did know which hen laid which egg. But Mendel would have been rather more than mildly surprised if he'd seen the results of Sammy's breeding programmes.

He put Lionel Rose in with my trousered bantie hens, and we got black, white, and black-and-white chicks, long trousers, pedal pushers, or shorts.

They were yellow and black to start with, but by the time the fluff turned to feathers they were all stalking round the yard beating up Chickenheart offspring, and giving their poor mother the vapours. He crossed chooks and bantams in every conceivable colour variation, and a few inconceivable ones. Any size, any colour. You name it, we had it.

Mother was a stout, busy little chook-bantam-cross hen, and as far as I can see she perpetually sat on eggs or raised chickens. I do not recall ever seeing her without a batch of chirping children and Sammy claims she never lost an egg. She was the perfect mother, and while every other hen was indifferent to the egg-stealing antics of Mechanic, a four-foot-long, rough-tail goanna who lived in the garage and strolled over to the bough-shed occasionally for a tid-bit, Mother always attacked him fiercely whenever she chanced to meet him.

She once raised twelve lusty white leghorn children who nightly cuddled under and over her in the back of a tea-chest until she left them for a new batch of eggs, and henceforth refused to acknowledge their existence. But they could not forget her, and sought solace nightly in the tea-chest long after they should have been scuffling for places on the perches.

The situation became ludicrous, as they waxed larger and fatter — twelve great chooks crammed themselves nightly into the tea-chest with squawks and shoves and feathers flying and were most upset when Sammy finally removed the tea-chest. They packed themselves into a pile where it had lain, and refused to shift. He had to put up a perch above the spot and lift them on to it one by one every night for a week.

Once I had to send Joe a chook telegram. Mandy, at six, had discovered and kept secret the fact that one of Sammy's hens had chosen an independent course of action and laid a clutch of eggs at the bottom of an empty, upright forty-four gallon drum behind the new shed.

Mandy inspected her "setty hen" daily and fed her tid-bits; she too was going to be the owner of some chickens, and maybe a champion fighting cock.

We were on our way to town in the car when suddenly Mandy gasped "My setty hen!" and burst into tears. "It's nearly twenty-one days — they'll hatch while I'm in town, and the chickies won't be able to get out, and they'll all die in the drum," she wept.

I consoled her that I'd send Dad a telegram to rescue them. The lengthy explanations and instructions where to find them were dispatched as soon as we reached town. As all telegrams may be heard by anyone listening to the session, I pictured the raised eyebrows of those who heard my 'pregnant chook in drum' message go out over the air waves.

The bolt-drum twins were another abberation from the norm of fowl-raising. On a low shelf in the workshop an errant hen laid two eggs in a twelve-gallon drum, three-quarters filled with gutter-bolts.

It was December, and stinking hot day and night. The eggs hatched without hen-help, and two motherless yellow chicks emerged. Probably someone tried to introduce them to the chook-house, but the drum of gutter-bolts was home, and the workshop their run, with water in the dog-dish under the tap at the end of the shed, and a plentiful supply of insects at all times.

Because it was too hot to work in the shed during the day, Joe worked there after tea until about eleven, and the light attracted the insects in myriads.

The twins leapt off their bed of bolts and gorged on moths and flying creatures. They were both roosters, and they grew enormous. Unless their mother had had an affair with an emu, the only explanation for their size has to be the rich diet of night moths added to the daytime insects.

Joe said it was quite disconcerting to become suddenly aware of two pairs of beady eyes watching him on a level with the bench he was working on.

Fitting themselves back into the drum of bolts to sleep became increasingly difficult.

The most unusual thing about the twins was that they appeared to have but one brain between the two of them. What one did the other did. They always moved side by side, and if one turned its head to the left; the other turned its head to the left; if one stopped short, the other stopped short. They didn't act like chooks at all. They ran together in short, sharp bursts, stopped together, veered together.

Maybe it was because of their orphaned chickenhood, with no mother to train and comfort them. They looked to each other for instructions, but neither had the ability to take the lead.

We were slightly ashamed of them as they began to move further afield from the workshop and to catch the eye of our occasional visitors.

"What's wrong with those roosters?" they'd say curiously, as the twins would appear shoulder to shoulder, darting forward six feet, stopping, darting a yard to the left, stopping, darting on again, until they'd zig-zagged out of sight. "Oh, nothing," we'd say, and change the subject.

We had a visitor once who owned the most modern of fowl-raising establishments near Sydney. Sammy proudly escorted him to the bough-shed.

He said he couldn't believe his own eyes; he roared with laughter; he said, well he supposed they must be the happiest chooks he'd ever be likely to meet.

Sammy felt sorry for him because all his chooks were white leghorns and it must be terribly difficult to tell them apart, and to make up to him a little Sammy called out Cassius and Lionel for an exhibition spar.

We always had plenty of eggs, but it was another matter altogether to extort table poultry from my chook-boy. The only time I pulled rank and ordered a plump fowl to the axe, the meal was a dismal failure.

"You know that's Hector, don't you?" said Sammy accusingly, whereupon Mandy started to snivel, and Pete wailed in sympathy. With three bawling kids refusing to eat poor Hector, I suddenly didn't feel like any myself.

Then we had the mouse plague, followed by the rat plague, followed by the cat plague. When the cats had finished the rats, they turned on the chooks. No matter what we did, those feral cats got into the chook-house nightly, and stalked the chooks by day when they wandered in the surrounding scrub.

The chooks took to the trees, and learned to fly from branch to branch as the cats pounced. The bough-shed was so large that about six trees grew up through the spinifex roof, and in their branches the chooks sought refuge.

They eschewed the use of nests in boxes on the ground, and made their own on the roof. We had arborial chooks, and collecting the eggs was a hazardous undertaking, as kids swarmed up and crawled over the spinifex, and eggs plopped through the thin patches and splattered below.

An outburst of squawks from the chook-house trees was the signal for the schoolroom door to burst open and kids with shanghais to speed to the rescue, but still the slaughter continued.

By the time the cats moved on, only about a sixth of Sammy's chooks remained.

Cassius and Sonny and Chickenheart were gone, and Mother's little pen was empty and silent. A subdued Sammy raked, cleaned, and repaired chookhouse and nests, but his heart was not in it. "I'm not going to breed any more chooks for the rotten cats to eat!" he stated firmly. "I think I'll get some ducks." And he did, but that's another story.

Outback driving:
'I think she means
the carby'

I don't claim to be one of those intrepid pioneer wives who accompanied their menfolk uncomplainingly into the never-never; I had to be hauled there, kicking and screaming.

Those women made their homes and bore their children and perhaps never saw another white woman for three years or more.

After three months I developed a tic in my left eye if I heard the word bullock; the mention of 'steers' made me twitch spasmodically; and a graphic description of 'lumpy-jaw' caused an uncontrollable out-burst of wild laughter.

Joe decided some female company might do me good. It was a pity the road was so bad, and so lonely, but if I carried the portable transceiver to contact the station if I did have any trouble, then maybe . . .

Within seconds I was hurling suitcases, children, tucker-box, transceiver, spare water, spare petrol, and my lucky black cat charm into the vehicle, and I was already gunning the motor when Joe yelled out, "Hey, seeing you're going to town you may as well take the welder in for repairs!"

It was the welder that did it. I negotiated the anthills and the salt lakes and the Deathtrap Sandhills, — 80 miles up in the first day, and a smug transceiver report from our first night's camp, with the prospect of a clear run on a better road the next day.

Midday next day — 320 miles behind me, and only 80 to go — and me chanting elatedly:

"NO more bullocks, no more steers,

Mention a mickie, and I'll box your ears"

when Clunk! clatter-clatter-clatter! The weight of the welder in the back of the station-wagon had buckled one of the back-wheel rims. I threw away the mangled bits, and put on the spare. But now a vague apprehension began to creep into my reckoning, and the long red ribbon of lonely road stretched ahead. 75 miles still to go, when Clunk! clitter-clatter-clatter! The other back-wheel rim had collapsed.

"It's a good thing we've got plenty of tucker," said Sammy morosely.

"I wanna go home to Daddy," wailed Mandy.

"This is the site for a village," announced smart-alec Melissa.

I threw a rock at her and rigged the transceiver.

If you have ever wondered what the subject of conversation is when two outback women meet, you need wonder no longer.

It is motor-vehicles, breakdowns of, and pet lists of what spares are a must to carry on bush roads.

No female blooded on our desert roads ever moves beyond the house-paddock without her supply of powdered milk (or Lactogen), her cake of soap, and her roll of fencing wire.

Where our grandmothers kept beautifully-written recipe books, and traded their prickly-pear-jam and wild-tomato-pickle secrets, we keep notebooks in the glove-box, not much to look at, begrimed with oily thumb-prints, but a treasury of informative advice, — for instance, what to feed the baby on when you've poured his lactogen into the radiator to stop the leak, or stupid questions to flatter the male ego so he'll do the job for you.

Until strict necessity ordained otherwise, my conception of a motor-car included only exterior appearance and the convenience of the cushioned interior.

To lift up the bonnet was, to me, something akin to doing a post-mortem on a cadaver: all sorts of nasty things were exposed, and only a genius could work out which one was the cause of the breakdown. Even after I overcame my abhorrence of exposing the vehicle's innards to the light of day, I could never remember the correct terminology for the various organs and intestines.

This may not have been so bad if I had not been forced to reveal my ignorance to the world at large, when I rigged the transceiver and called for advice.

Joe knew what I meant when I referred to the little round hat-thing with hoses sticking out of it, or the big block-thing with the hole in the top, but at times even he was puzzled by my descriptions, and often helpful voices hundreds of miles away chipped in with "I think she means the carby, Joe," or "Sounds like she's out of oil. "

I was always grateful for advice from anyone, but it made me feel somehow inadequate.

There was one area, however, where I held my own.

There was, on our road to town about 60 miles from the homestead, a stretch of about three miles of extremely nasty sandhills bordering a quicksand salt-lake (known as Lake Salt Beef, on account of having swallowed up sixty head of thirst-crazed cattle from a drover's mob one moonlit night.)

The kids called this stretch The Deathtrap Sandhills, and rarely a traveller escaped their clutches at some time or another. If they missed him going, they usually got him coming back.

The sandhills stretched right to the shores of Lake Salt Beef, and a forty-mile detour was the only way to avoid them. I was careful to tackle this stretch only in the early morning or the late afternoon, but on the return journey this always meant that I was driving straight west into the setting sun, which meant that I couldn't see the track properly, and steered by the wind-row.

I'd yell "Hang on tight!" to the kids, put the car into second, and hurl the vehicle as fast as I could at the twisting track, with engine roaring.

We leapt, swerved, and bucketed along, but I knew if I slowed down for the curves, we'd get stuck, so it was always touch-and-go whether we skidded off the track and ended up with the front end of the car buried up to the windscreen in a sandbank.

All the men would tell me frequently how I OUGHT to drive, but I always forgot their instructions at the crucial moment, and roared in with gritted teeth, albeit petrified with fright.

Our elderly station-wagon, fondly known as Decibel after the exhaust pipe fell off, always did the right thing and got us through, and on one occasion she actually drove herself.

She was old, three of the four doors were roped shut due to exhausted locks, and the rear-vision mirror frequently slipped and reflected a clear view of the back of the front seat.

On this particular trip I was unaware that Sammy had acquired in town a shoe-box housing six white mice. In the back seat, he and Mandy, bored with travelling since dawn, and solicitous of the mice's welfare, were extracting them one by one and feeding them on biscuit crumbs.

At the point where I yelled "Hang on, kids," Sammy was holding a mouse. As he explained later, it was not possible to hang on, the way I drove, and hold a mouse at the same time. Therefore he opened his hand, and the mouse jumped for the nearest object, which was the back of the front seat.

As we slid, lurched, and catapulted along, with a great cloud of white sand mushrooming out behind us, a slight movement registered in the slipped rear-vision mirror. I've got ambidextrous eyes: I kept one on the wind-row and the other on the mouse which, despite the way it was sliding and scrambling for a hold, was approaching my left shoulder. It was twitching its whiskers, and had a distinctly terror-stricken expression, but, good grief, what do you think I had!

A wilder skid than usual must have un-nerved the mouse, for he leapt again, this time on to my shoulder. I took both hands off the wheel, beat at him with one, and tried to open the door to jump out with the other, but it was one of the roped-shut doors, so the escape route was barred.

The mouse then ran round the back of my neck, and got out of my line of vision.

I calmed down a bit when I couldn't see him, and it might have been all right if he hadn't reached up and bitten me on the ear. And hung on! I suppose it was the kids screaming that frightened him.

My foot was flat on the accelerator, and we were almost airborne. I got a grip on the mouse and wrenched him off my ear just as Decibel speared through the last of the sand and hit a hard ridge in the road; which catapulted the mouse on to the top of my head, where it slipped, scrabbled, loosened my upswept hairdo, and fell, swinging like a pendulum on a long strand of hair at about the level of my chin.

I braked: Decibel stopped. There was dead silence. The only movement was made by the slowly-gyrating mouse.

Tentatively, Mandy reached cut a little hand and steadied the mouse: it was trembling with shock. Slowly, Sammy took out his pocket-knife, reached up and sawed off a dollar's worth of my town hair-do. Then he put the mouse, complete with my lock of hair, back in the shoe-box, and we proceeded home.

I always used to get my hair set in town the day before I left, because I wanted Joe to see what I could look like if I really tried. I hadn't even had a hair-set on my wedding day, because we got married at short notice at a race-meeting.

But because of the sort of breakdowns I had, I always used to arrive home with my hair looking like a rat's nest, and on one occasion, as I have related, like a mouse's nest.

Decibel never broke the same thing twice. Sammy said that was a good thing, because each time I learned something new, which would stand me in good stead if I ever got REALLY stuck somewhere.

But quite often this lack of prior experience resulted in my pulling off bits which I needn't have pulled off, with much grease and oil and tearing of hair.

Like taking the carby to pieces and washing it out with petrol, when the only thing wrong was that the kids had only half-filled the fuel tank when I thought they'd filled it, so I was out of fuel. You couldn't tell from the fuel gauge, because it wasn't working.

Refuelling was one of the things I disliked most. I had to hoist a jerry-can on to the roof of the car, stick a piece of hose into the can and suck till the petrol came down the hose. I used to suck till I was blue in the face, and nothing would happen, and then it would flow suddenly and I'd get a mouthful of petrol. What a relief when I discovered that the kids could all do it easily, one suck and hey presto.

All my friends had similar experiences. My mouse was nothing compared to Mary-Anne's goat. Somebody gave her a saanen for milk for the baby, but I still think she shouldn't have tried to take it home in the back seat of the car. Not a brand-new car, anyway. However, I think her husband over-reacted when he snatched up a .22 and shot the goat.

Rural reading,
'riting and
'rithmatic

Rural reading, 'riting and 'rithmatic

If you think you have problems now with primary correspondence education, that's only the shower to toughen you up before the storm, and in some cases the cyclone, of secondary education.

Sammy and Melissa have finished grade seven, so gird your loins, Mum, AND Dad. The first hurdle is the uniform. Sammy, with a carefree childhood behind him where only bare feet and elastic sides figure, has now to be introduced to shoes, and shoes all day and seven days a week. Mums who can put up with the whingeing, buy a pair and make him wear them on Sunday afternoons during the holidays. When the whingeing subsides a bit, tell him about ties, but leave the school to make him wear one. Melissa, in the meantime, has to know about gloves and school hats, and Melissa is going to whinge about four times as long as Sammy: there's nothing you can do about it, except make your mind a blank, and say "yes dear," at intervals, but be ready to pick up the changed note in the voice when she says "you don't love me any more, do you?" so that you give the right answer.

Sammy started grade one with his little black mate, Frankie, and has refused point-blank to go to boarding school unless Frankie goes too, on the grounds that mates have to share the bad times as well as the good. So you've done all the explaining to his parents, and applied for the grants, and organised the paperwork, and Frankie is going too. Frankie doesn't whinge: he gives you a big white-toothed grin, so maybe he'll help Sammy through.

He'll help him all right! It's three weeks after you've said goodbye to them at school eight hundred miles away, and here comes the mail-truck, and my god isn't that Sammy and Frankie sitting up on the load on the back!

They're dirty, and their clothes are dirty, and they're barefooted, and they've walked and hitched rides until they met the mailman 200 miles back. It's not a fit place for a kid, Mum, the headmaster belted them. Why did the headmaster belt them? Well, they were starving, absolutely dying of starvation, and there was no bush tucker in the benighted place, but they were lucky enough to do what they'd often done out bush at home: they caught a cat. A big boy saw the fire they made, and pimped on them, and the headmaster belted hell out of them, and said some terrible things, and Frankie said why don't we go home.

Dad has a talk to them, and Dad drives them back, but Mum's job is the hardest. You try writing a letter to the headmaster apologising for your son and his mate eating the school cat!

Sammy thinks Dad is the greatest, and he models himself on Dad whenever he can. Dad has an idiosyncrasy about filling in forms; he claims it is an invasion of privacy, and he delights in filling in ridiculous answers for far-away government departments down south: often the family help him, and many an evening has been whiled away with the family volunteering ludicrous answers for Dad to fill in. Sammy meets his first form; it's an IQ test, and he fills it in according to family tradition. He comes out with an IQ of 25, but the family doesn't know this, and the first semester reports come home. Frankie's is a bobby-dazzler, but the main thing on Sammy's is comment G, which reads: Doing as well as can be expected under special circumstances.

Questioning Sammy reveals that they don't make him do much work; he's allowed to sit in the back of the class and draw pictures, and he doesn't have to do the tests, but sometimes he gets bored with drawing pictures and listens to the teacher, anyway.

So you have to take them back to school, Mum, and see the headmaster about Sammy. He looks very doubtful when you insist that Sammy do the normal work, and you suspect that he's trying to tell you Sammy is dumb without actually putting it into words. He adds very brightly that Sammy is a star at football. You stand your ground and he gives in reluctantly, and you go away feeling there's something funny somewhere because you taught Sammy for seven years and you KNOW he's rather bright. You don't wake up until about three years later when Sammy happens to mention during a family form-filling-in evening that he'd had great fun with his own first form.

Then there's Letters Home. These can be the hardest cross of all for a poor mother. It's not Sammy's, it's Melissa's. Sammy's first letter will read:

Dear Mum and Dad,

The first eleven won 2-nil. The second eleven lost 2-3. The third eleven won 9-6. The bubs won 3-nil. The picture on Saturday was Dr Jekyl and Mr Hyde. I get the stitches out on Monday.

Your loving son, Sam.

PS. Send five dollars.

The second and all the ensuing letters will be just the same, except for the changed football scores and picture title. Where Sammy's letter is a scant half page, Melissa will fill five or six tearful pages. She cannot bear to be parted from her darling baby brother. She lies awake every night thinking how her pony and her dog will be fretting for her. She has no friends, and the girls are all horrid, and the mistresses are all pigs.

Your only comfort here is that a child who can write such evocative prose is certain to get an A for English, but it doesn't help much if you've got a limp, dejected dog whimpering on the verandah, and a limp, dejected pony whimpering at the house gate. All you can do is go into the bedroom and have a whimper yourself, and then go and take another photo of the pony for her in one of its less dejected moments.

Melissa's letters will change, of course. By her second year she will have learned all about cosmetics and fashions from the more sophisticated girls, and unless you're forewarned, she's going to play merry hell with your charge account at the big store when they let her out for Saturday shopping. She will start her letter by telling you what a lovely mum she's got, and how she loves you, and she knows it did cost rather a lot, but you wouldn't want her to be a frump beside the other girls, would you, etc. etc. Pony and dog will be relegated to the last paragraph, or even a PS. There will be lots of other news, which you'll enjoy reading, and the A for English is still assured.

There is a way around the charge account problem. When she comes home for the holidays, you explain that now she's growing up she should have a clothes allowance, and you discuss how much it should be in front of Dad, who'll put the brakes on at your previously-arranged amount. In case she hasn't assimilated that the charge account is now taboo, you write to the store to that effect.

Melissa comes home by plane, and she comes home a week earlier than Sammy every holidays. The schools are in different States, so you don't really begin to puzzle about it until Sammy complains and draws your attention to it. You have not realised the depths of cunning and subterfuge to which a really determined little girl can descend. Melissa has sized up and tested out her school's staff and found out that not one of these urban-based ladies knows the slightest thing about the outback. She can tell them anything, and she knows just how far to go. She knows they can check the plane as far as Alice Springs, but after that she has them on the hip. She consults her calendar, and invents monthly mail-runs, and private contractors, and connecting stops by desert anthills on a date which is always one week before the school breaks up. The dopes fall for it.

There is absolutely no way to write a letter to a headmistress, telling them your daughter has been making fools of them for the last three years.

The one date you are sure of is the date when they must go back after the Christmas holidays, because it's the Wet.

Two days before departure day, the kids are going to start putting the pressure on to stay home, and Sammy and Frankie will bribe the tribe's rainmaker with tobacco they've pinched from the store to "sing 'im up big rain", to put the road out. You will be sorely tempted because it is going to be harder for you to get used to the empty homestead again than it will be for them to go back. You pause. You know you're just being selfish. Then Melissa puts a record on in the lounge, a teenage taste record, and the decibels slam you up against the kitchen cupboard, and Sammy puts on his cassette player on the verandah in opposition, and the walls vibrate, and the floors vibrate.

"Goodbye kids. Have a good trip. See you next holidays!"

Taking on the big city lights

There comes a time in every bushie's life when he or she goes away for a holiday.

It might be a mighty long time coming, but, eventually, come it does.

And the plans! The city-life for a spell; the old friends to greet; the theatres; the kids can see a museum, art galleries, toy shops; and they can meet the grandparents again, who haven't seen them since they were mere toddlers.

After the eight-year drought was over, the bank manager let us take a holiday in Perth. There was even enough cash for me to make a determined assault on the dress-goods shelf in the hawker's van, and with the aid of the fashion pages in the magazines, I sewed for weeks and produced our city wardrobes.

Isn't it funny how the expectation always seems to outdo the actual event!

Before we left I spent hours imagining how impressed Nana and Pop were going to be by my beautiful children.

Well, I know the kids spent a great deal of their time with the house-girls and the piccaninnies; all bush kids do. They were bi-lingual; they could track; they could find bush-tucker. But that's no reason why Sammy and Melissa had to walk behind us across the tarmac carrying their airways bags on their heads.

Mandy, at four, could speak perfectly good English; I could never fathom why she chose to speak nothing but Wailbri for the whole six weeks of our stay.

I guess Pete was our only success; at 18 months he charmed Nana, and he wasn't allergic to whatever it was that brought the other three out in itchy lumps and runny noses.

We didn't get out much, because the housekeeper was apprehensive about baby-sitting; she claimed that she felt that odd child, Mandy, was swearing at her in that funny lingo.

Sammy explained earnestly before I could stop him just what she was saying, which translated roughly as "fat woman with many creeks in the face needs bowel-motion to improve temperament." THAT wasn't a very pleasant evening!

On the few occasions when we were able to leave the children and indulge in the city social life, my clothes were all wrong. That hawker had lied to me — his materials weren't the very latest from Sydney. They were probably the rejects from the days when his grandfather carted them up the Birdsville Track on a camel-pack.

And I defy any wife not to feel hurt when her husband arranges behind her back for her glamorous city girl-friend to take her shopping for a 'smart outfit', AND gives the cheque to the girlfriend!

It took me quite a while to persuade Alicia, but once she agreed, we had a great time. But she wouldn't stay while I modelled our purchases for my beloved. He said it was an expensive way to get my point across, and he was relieved to hear I didn't intend to go public, because he didn't think he had enough money to pay the fine for soliciting, as well as pay for the second-hand station wagon he was going to buy tomorrow to take us all back where we belonged.

Even our exit from the city didn't go according to plan. The city fathers had just built a new bridge across the Narrows, and we had to drive past it on our way into the city.

As an ex-resident of that beautiful city, I was naturally assigned the job of navigator, but suddenly, instead of one road, there were dozens, with arrows and signs everywhere. We found ourselves not passing, but on, the bridge. Left lanes, right lanes, signs! We got off the bridge, and had another go. On the bridge again. Off again.

Sammy and Melissa shrieked their versions of the right way to go, and Mandy swore in Wailbri. Three times we did it, and then Joe gave up and drove right across to the suburb on the other side of the river, and pulled up and snatched the map from me.

A nice policeman on a motorbike came up to tell us we couldn't park there, but when Joe explained, he looked sympathetic, and said "Follow me, mate," and escorted us right to the causeway we'd been heading for originally.

Probably the best part of a holiday is telling your friends about it afterwards; they've usually experienced the culture-clash too, and you can swap anecdotes. It only takes one experience to learn that small children always behave much better on their home ground, so you can always repair any misconceptions by inviting grandparents to observe the children in their own environment.

When in the city a bushman must try to follow the adage 'when in Rome do as the Romans do', or, at least, when observing the Romans at play, keep a still tongue in his head until he gets back to his ground.

Some of the Romans' political beliefs may not meet with his, but that is no excuse to start a fight in the saloon bar.

For the ringer or prospector making a first visit to the great metropolis a few words of warning. Buy a map of the city; you can't tell your direction from the sun. It rains often down there, and the sky is cloudy more often than not. You can't tell it from the stars either because the illumination from the street lights blots them out. And even if you could, the buildings get in the way, and you can't follow a bee-line. Apart from that, there's the dog-droppings. In some places it's not safe to take your eyes off the footpath unless you're standing still.

Permissive society or not, you're likely to get your face slapped if you tell a girl she'd be worth six dogs in a man's swag.

Study up the local idiom, and try to avoid using the verbs to camp, to plant, and to bogey. In the city the first means to take a tent and sleep inside it on a stretcher; the second means to dig a hole in the garden and put seeds or seedlings in it; and the third doesn't exist. The equivalents you must use are to sleep, to hide, and to wash. Practise these substitutions for a couple of weeks before you go down inside, — as you were — before you go to the city.

The Roman con-men are experts at parting a fool from his money, and if you don't think you are a fool, you should prove it by paying your hotel bill in advance, and purchasing your return ticket before you do anything else. One erstwhile, well-heeled young drover I knew had to go five rounds with a 6'6" American negro in a seaside boxing booth to get his train fare for the Ghan, so he could return to his job.

Someone ought to write one of those How to Do It books with advice for bush people on how to avoid getting into arguments when visiting the city. I'm not the one to do it, though, because, despite all my good intentions, I always seem to end up in what, at best, might be termed 'heated discussions.'

Airways personnel, elderly aunties, old biddies on buses, patronising professors, and even, no, mostly, earnest student offspring of the friends of my youth; they all invariably hit me at some stage early in the conversation with the modern version of 'Wot about the workers?'

This, of course, implies that I am not a worker, which tends to irritate me slightly. It usually devolves that the generally accepted view is that no pastoralist is considered a worker.

Among the more rabid university types the commonly held picture seems to be a cross between a brutal giant in a wide hat plying a whip over the backs of a group of cowering Aborigines, a straw-chewing halfwit, and a corpulent cattle-baron dropping rocks on sacred sites from his second-best Cessna.

At a recent Melbourne party I tried to remind myself that they all really meant well, as I sipped my first drink. Yuk! Dandelion wine! Somebody offered me a plate, and I realised with horror that my hostess and fellow-guests were into their vegetarian phase, and nobody had warned me.

At this stage I had a presentiment that it would probably be in the best interests of all concerned if I invented an excuse and left quickly.

I slunk into the Ladies to fabricate a reasonable story, and was tossing up between a migraine and a burst appendix when my sanctuary was invaded by a toothy female with very definite ideas on animal liberation, which in no way coincided with mine on the subject. I fled back into the lounge and rapidly disposed of two glasses of dandelion wine.

It's a pity some plant liberationist hadn't liberated those dandelions before my hostess' son rammed them into a bottle; it would have been a calmer evening if he had.

My first Yuk impression was wrong. Those dandelions had hairs on their chests. I savoured the bouquet. I categorised the wine as subtle but insistent, perhaps a mite sneaky.

It sneaked up on me and revealed an aggressive quality which suggested its progenitors might well have sprung forth in the garden of Attila the Hun. It had a definite clout! I drank two more glasses quickly, and shoved the bottle down behind the divan. The greenery we were supposed to eat didn't appeal to me, so 1 decided to stick to my flower-power.

A weedy little hairy man came and sat beside me, carrying a bowl of what looked like indigofera in white sauce, which he proceeded to ladle into his mouth between staccato bursts of political propaganda which seemed not at all sympathetic to the interests of the pastoral industry.

He asked me what I thought. At that stage I was too polite to tell him. I fished around behind the divan and liberated another battalion of dandelion guerillas into my glass.

He seized a stick of celery from a passing tray, and brandished it under my nose to emphasise his statement, "You cattle barons are all the same!" The tray was still hovering about, so I grabbed a stick too, and poked him in the chest with it.

"Baroness, my good man," I stated firmly. "Your erroneous impression as to my sex is about as valid as your uninformed political beliefs."

When he opened his mouth to reply I stuck my stick of celery horizontally between his teeth, rose haughtily, and marched into the kitchen for another bottle of dandelion volcano.

Then I went looking for some animal-libbers to straighten out. It was then an easy step to smarten up a couple of misinformed lecturers and a woman lawyer with distorted views on the part played by primary industry in the Australian economy.

My dandelions and I were invincible. They attacked, but we parried; we charged! Confrontation was meat, drink, and fertiliser to us. We were no longer polite, and we told them what we thought on any subject they liked to mention, plus a few we thought up for ourselves.

In retrospect I thoroughly enjoyed my Melbourne party, but I don't think I furthered the cause of Farmlink very much. Perhaps it would be as well if I planned my next holiday for Cape York Peninsula.

The Christmas
cooking pot

The Christmas cooking pot

The drought had been going on for so long that when Pete started school on correspondence lessons and read about green grass, he thought the book was nuts, because everyone should know that grass is brown. That was about the same time that we had the tinned-dog Christmas.

Not that you could blame Fred and me; we did our best. We'd been living on tinned meat for so long that if we could have flattened out the tins we could have built another shed on the station. We must have been the most meat-hungry family in Australia.

About a week before Christmas Mum started to hint about a killer. Dad was pretty touchy those days. He went to some lengths to explain that the cattle that weren't already dead were so poor that you couldn't possibly eat the meat if you were starving yourself, which as far as he could see we weren't; that the cattle of his three neighbours — who were all hawk-eyed b-s, anyway — were just as scrawny as ours; and that if we thought he was going to town before Christmas to chuck money about like a fool we could have another think. If he showed his nose out of the scrub and the agents spotted him, it would probably remind them to sell us up, and we wouldn't even have a home for Christmas, let-alone a killer.

He got real worked-up. Mum wasn't game to say a word, but that night for tea we got the tinned-dog plain, without even any onions.

It was only a couple of days before Christmas that Fred got his idea. Dad had gone out to pull a bore down the other end of the run, and we were sitting in the shed just lazing about, when Fred's eyes lit on the old motorbike.

"Gee," he said, "I know how we can get a killer for Christmas. I saw a couple of roos yesterday, up past the end of the air-strip. I'll take the bike and see if I can start 'em up and head 'em this way, and you go and get the twenty-two, and when they get close enough, you bag one. Fresh meat — yippee!"

It sounded a good idea to me. We were so hungry for fresh meat anything was a good idea. How were we to know what was going to happen?

Fred roared off on the bike, and I sneaked into Dad's office and got the gun. I could hear Mum and Mandy talking in the kitchen, but they didn't hear me, so I nipped out and planted behind the shed.

Fred told me afterwards that he had only gone about three miles when he spotted the kangaroos' tracks. There were two of them lying in the shade of a scraggy tree, and when they heard the bike they jumped up. One shot off into the scrub straight away, but the other paused just long enough to give Fred time to cut off its retreat, and he revved the bike up, and got that roo pointed in the general direction of the airstrip before it had time to scratch itself.

Then off it went like a jet. When it got to the strip it tried to cut across, but Fred hazed it back, though the bike nearly pelted him when he ran into a melon hole. But he kept her going and there was this roo coming straight down the strip towards the shed. I started to yell encouragement and then I saw Mandy come out the back door with a bucket in her hand heading for the tank.

About two hundred yards to go, and my finger was itching on the trigger, and Mandy was standing by the tank with her mouth hanging open.

Just then the roo made a last wild attempt to dodge. He swung around, and there was the bike, coming full-pelt at him. He gave a leap clean over Fred and the bike, but Fred wheeled that bike on a five cent piece, and though we couldn't see it for a cloud of dust, Fred reckoned he ran over the roo's tail when he turned him again. Anyway, out of this mighty cloud of dust comes the roo, over the fence in one leap, and into the yard. Fred said later that he didn't see the fence for the dust, but the bike hit it, and this time it did pelt him.

Mandy was screaming, and I was yelling to her to get out of the way. Our killer had gone straight into a sheet on the clothes-line, and had got itself wrapped up in it, and was turning cartwheels towards the tank-stand. Fred was sitting up, yelling to me to shoot, and Mandy was dodging round and round the tank-stand waving the bucket, while the roo got himself neatly wedged between the house and the tank.

I saw a great claw come through the sheet and rip it down, and the tail swung round and knocked Mandy clear. I reckoned where the head would be and pulled the trigger. The sun must have got in my eyes or something. The next minute there's this neat little hole in the tank and the water's pouring out. And there's the roo, still wearing the remains of the sheet, over the back fence and going like a jet across the flat.

I guess it was because of all the yelling that we hadn't heard Dad come back in the truck for some extra gear he needed. Fred and I spotted him together. The bike was still lying on its side, chugging away, and Fred picked it up and was on it like a shot. I raced across the yard, chucking the gun down as I went, and when I jumped the fence I bet I went higher than the roo did. I hit the pillion and we left fast. Dad is a short-tempered man.

We went about eight miles down the road and stayed there until it got pretty late. Then we decided there was nothing for it but to go home. Fred said he didn't much feel like riding the bike, so this time he got on the pillion, and we started off, both of us feeling pretty low.

Only about a mile from home, and Fred leans forward and says in my ear: "Sam, a man's got a second chance. Look there! Poultry!"

There are times when you don't stop to think. You just act. I saw the emu, and I revved the bike. The emu started to run. It was only about five yards off the road, and the faster I went the faster it went. Half a mile down the road it paced us, heading straight for the house and the cooking pot. We were going to redeem ourselves by really bringing in a Christmas killer this time. We would have, too, if that dumb bird hadn't swerved and tried to cut across in front of me.

We must have been doing forty miles an hour, and it's doing the same, and the next minute there it is, slanting straight in towards me. I just have time to throw out my arm, and somehow I grab it round the neck and hold it off. I can't let go or it will crash into us, and I can't slow down either, because that's the hand I want for the throttle. Fred's hanging on to me, and I'm hanging on to the emu, and I don't know whether the bike's towing the emu, or the emu's towing the bike. But what I do know is that Dad's out in the yard, because I can hear him yelling.

My arm's aching like mad, holding off that bird, but all I can think of is that we've got to keep going until we run out of petrol. And 1 hope it's not going to be long, because it's getting on towards dark and there's no way in the world I'm going to be able to switch on the light. I read somewhere that an emu can only run a short distance at high speed but it's a lie. As we whizzed past the house Dad was roaring like a scrub bull, and he must have frightened the emu more than he did us, because it put on an extra spurt and I'll swear we touched fifty.

Fred was hanging on to the back of my shirt, and he kept saying over and over — "the square on the hypotenuse of a right-angled triangle is equal to the sum of the squares on the other two sides" — which wasn't much help to me. He said afterwards that he couldn't possibly have said that because he didn't even know it when he was at school. But he said it all right, about fifty times, and when we went past Dad he was shouting it. My mind had just about gone blank, when suddenly I felt the neck go wobbly in my grasp and the beak hit my thumb with a bump. I let go quick, grabbed the throttle, and swerved sideways. I stopped the bike, and Fred fell off the back, and my knees started to shake. Not because of the ride, but because I could see Dad coming full bore down the road after us in the truck.

The emu was staggering and weaving round the road in front of us. Fred jumped up and made a dive for him. I must say he was single-minded about that Christmas killer. But the emu must have got his second wind once my hand was no longer strangling him. He took one great stride past Fred's crouching form, and lit out again down the road, and I bet he didn't stop until he reached the West Australian border.

That was the worst Christmas Fred and I ever had. Mum made a pudding and Mandy iced a flash Christmas cake, and we had a nice salad with the cold tinned-dog. But Dad kept saying "Have some more poultry, boys!" or "Now, who'd like a nice roo steak?"

Mandy and Pete giggled so much it made a fellow feel like leaving home.

Putting the
is a flaming

It is the trendy thing at present to dredge up, explore, and label as problems, the incidental by-products of any way-of-life.

I propose therefore to reveal a hitherto-neglected area in which many a bush housewife is exposed to traumatic experiences of extreme magnitude. I refer, of

pressure on
nuisance

course, to the first time she is left at the homestead alone, absolutely alone, tens or even hundreds of miles from her nearest neighbour.

She is probably in her early twenties, enthusiastic, and keen to show him that she is a capable and efficient help-mate, and to give the lie to all those old biddies who insinuate that a bush boy is asking for trouble by marrying a city-bred girl.

He kisses her goodbye and says he'll be back Thursday. She waves from the gate until he is out of sight, and then, as she is about to go inside, she suddenly notices just how immense and empty the surrounding landscape has grown. A tiny glimmer of apprehension creeps into her consciousness, but she shrugs it off and goes inside, like the brave "woman of the west" she intends to become.

I got through the first afternoon, but I came to grief at sundown. I'd forgotten to ask him how to light the pressure lamp. I knew you poured metho into it somewhere and then pumped it. So I stood it on the kitchen table in the half-light, and found the little pan, and I poured in the metho. Quite a bit of it slopped out of the pan, but I pressed on and, unaware that I should wait until the metho burned down, I pumped enthusiastically.

The whole affair immediately burst into leaping flames.

The kitchen curtains were perilously near. Fire — what to do?

Quench — extinguish — water, of course! I rushed out to the laundry, grabbed a bucketful, and heaved it from the kitchen doorway.

The resultant explosion would have gladdened the heart of a pyromaniac. No, I didn't burn the house down, but I don't ever want to repeat that hectic ten minutes, during which I reduced my beautiful kitchen to a reasonable facsimile of the aftermath of a cyclone.

The Australian outback doesn't dither around with long-drawn-out twilights. One minute you can see, and the next it's pitch dark. So when I retreated, panting, and still twitching with fright, to the verandah — which, for all I knew, was seething with taipans and death-adders — I was further assaulted by the realisation that he'd taken our only torch.

But for the regular drip, drip, emanating from the kitchen, all was silent. In lighted kitchens all over the land happy laughter, the clatter of crockery, and the tinkle of teaspoons; but not for me. For me, only this ominous silence, and a blackness inhabited by God-knows-what!

Actually it was curlews, but at the time I didn't know what they were, and I still adhere to the belief that there is no more eerie sound in the bush than the wail of a curlew in full throat on a moonless night.

I went through the process known as "pulling-yourself-together" and decided to emulate Scarlett O'Hara and "worry about it tomorrow". I'd lost all appetite, even if it had been possible to locate anything edible in that dark and dripping kitchen, so I sneaked cautiously along the verandah to the sanctuary of a bed, and crept into it, fully clothed — but not to sleep.

The silence was punctuated at intervals by the eldritch cries of curlews, and I'd barely adjusted to that, when a petrol drum contracted with a noise like a pistol shot. I'd heard that before, but it didn't stop me shrieking aloud. I simmered down. Another curlew, then the iron roof started cracking; another curlew; a dingo, and an answering dingo; two petrol drums in rapid succession; a long, whispering rustling; footsteps — FOOTSTEPS! Wild black fellows — rapists — psychopathic killers escaped from jail! I sat up in bed and yelled, and Boxer jumped up on the bed and licked my face.

Well, that was my first night alone, but it's only a mere shadow to what some of the girls have gone through.

Alison mastered the pressure lamp, and fed the assorted stock, and settled down to write letters after tea. Which was pretty difficult with the determined attacks of kami-kaze insect units attempting to immolate themselves on the lamp. But anyone experienced with lamps on a summer evening is accustomed to gnats, beetles, moths, crickets, and bush cockroaches bashing themselves into a stupor against the lamp glass and falling stunned to the floor. It's the ensuing sequence of events that is sometimes disconcerting. The light attracts the insects, and the insects attract the frogs. The third step in the food chain was Alison's nemesis.

She had the kitchen door open because it was so appallingly hot. Three or four large green frogs appeared, and set-to upon the insect banquet. This was routine evening entertainment — up until the point where the snake slithered in and seized Frog A, who shrieked piercingly, but not as piercingly as Alison. Frog B and Alison leapt for safety — Alison on to the kitchen table — and Frog C ignored the hullabaloo and phlegmatically ate another beetle. Frog C was taking a calculated risk, but his calculations were incorrectly based, and after the slow swallow of Frog A the snake then moved up on Frog C, who was positioned on the other side of the table from the doorway, thus opening up Alison's line of escape. Off the table, through the doorway, and up on the tankstand in creditable Olympic time.

But sitting all night on a tankstand is no pastime calculated to make for an amicable relationship between a bride of three months and the fellow who, she reasoned, was directly responsible for her predicament.

Edna possibly brought her trauma upon herself, but at that stage — six months married, three months pregnant — she wasn't to know that the worst thing you can do when you get a pain is to read the Home Doctor's Medical Book.

It was only a little pain, hardly a pain at all, possibly a slight touch of indigestion, but the silly girl, who probably would have ignored it had her loved one been there to distract her line of thought made what she thought was a logical assessment of cause and effect, and went for the doctor's book.

Even if you're not pregnant, or even if you're not a female, that book is positively R-rated for violence, and when you are 150 miles from a neighbour, at 9.30 at night, and the static on the transceiver is so violent that there is no way you are going to make contact with anyone, let alone a doctor, it can be an unnerving experience.

Edna looked up "Pregnancy", and by the time she turned the first page she was not only regretting her dewy-eyed plans for a large family, she was wishing heartily she'd never laid eyes on the fellow responsible for her condition.

She settled on "ectopic pregnancy". I quote "Ectopic gestation occurs when the ovum is arrested in the fallopian tube and begins to grow in this small cavity; such a condition is very serious indeed, and an operation is necessary to save the woman's life."

She dropped the book in fright, and another pain (a real one this time, she believed) smote her in the region of the abdomen. Well, she must accept this cruel blow of fate; there was nothing else she could do. By morning she would possibly be dying — alone — in the acutest of agonies, so while she was still capable of doing it she would write a farewell letter to her husband.

The first draft was formulated in a forgiving tone: "All our plans have come to naught, but it's not your fault, my darling," sort of thing. That would have been all right if Edna hadn't suddenly thought of the future, non-existent for her, but stretching probably another half century ahead for him. He was only 27; he'd get married again! Oh, would he, the stinker!

The second draft carried overtones of blame. She pointed out that it was he who had brought her to this benighted hole far from the haunts of other men (and specifically doctors) and the very least he could do was to remain celibate for the rest of his life in reparation for her untimely demise, and in order that some other unfortunate female would not be reduced to the suffering that was her lot.

On re-reading the missive, Edna felt that it was still not forceful enough under the circumstances. Draft 3 began: "You rotten, lousy pig," and covered three closely written pages. It was a gem of a farewell letter, a classic in vituperation, and an epic in imaginative ghostly reprisals.

Well satisfied, Edna glanced up at the clock, saw that it was one a.m., and registered that the pains had been absent for some three hours, so, exhausted by her efforts, she went to bed and slept soundly till morning.

After breakfast, she checked with the doctor on the medical session, was reassured, and then shamefacedly removed the letter from the mantelpiece and burned it, before hurrying to the kitchen to bake his favourite cake against her beloved's return. Imagine what a shattered marriage would have resulted if he'd ever read that letter. When you're alone never, never read a doctor's book. Even when you're bursting with health, and surrounded by family and friends, it's still taboo reading for anyone with the slightest fragment of imagination. Edna has five children and eight grandchildren now, and can cope with absolutely anything, but the events of that fearful night will always remain appallingly clear to her.

Such stories are legion, but in case any of the old biddies feel that my recital is a point in favour of their argument that city girls are out of place in the bush, just let them hold their fire, for fear of provoking me into revealing some of the side-splitting faux-pas committed by bush maidens on a first visit to the Big Smoke!

Bush races:
a flashback

I like bush race meetings: I got married at a race-meeting, and two of the kids were christened at race-meetings. I don't think they have them any more the way we used to. It was the big event of the year in the real outback. You worked like crazy seven days a week, 16 hours a day, for fifty-one weeks of the year, and then you took off one whole week and fitted a year's "play" into it.

For weeks beforehand everyone prepared for the races. The men paddocked their gun horses and exercised them on an improvised track at dawn, and the wives monitored their transceivers with vigilance, checking the telegram sessions to see whether any likely opponents were ordering feed (grass-fed meetings, corn-feeding against the rules) and listening in to the galah sessions for likely progress discussions on the neighbours' mounts and the favourite jockeys.

Let's take a flashback to any remote station back in the fifties.

The kids are training their ponies for the figure of eight and the barrel race, and Mum is ordering new clothes from the catalogue for herself and the kids, while teenage daughter is probably at the sewing machine in the sleepout making a daring ensemble for the Race Ball, which Mum is not going to let her wear, no way!

The excitement builds: there's one snag. Someone has to stay home and look after the place. The bookkeeper has been smart; he's secretary of the race club this year so he has to go. Mum always goes, because someone has to organise the tucker for the station's camp, and keep the kids in check. Dad's got the best horse he's had in years, and besides he stayed home last year because he had a broken ankle from a fall from a horse. What about the old fella — the cowboy butcher? He gets in the horrors on the first day of the races and misses all the fun, so he may as well stay home and miss the fun. Yeah, that's all very well, but after we've left there's sure to be some stragglers coming through late, who'll feel sorry for him and leave him a bottle of rum, and then he'll get in the horrors here, and defeat the purpose. Eldest son has a romance burgeoning by mail and message stick; he wants to consolidate it. Second son has starved himself down to eight stone seven, and is lined up to ride the champ. The ringers will give notice if they can't go.

Finally the cook solves the problem: he'll stay home for double pay and two weeks off to go to town after the races. He got a hiding at the races last year from a fellow who claimed Cookie had welshed on a bet, and the fellow will be there again this year, and likely to demand his money again when he's got a few under the belt.

It's settled then. The boys leave a week early to take the horses over, and refurbish the station's bough-shed camp with a new spinifex roof. Mum cooks vast quantities of salt beef, and the cook makes extra bread. The race club's been talking about getting a caterer for years, but it's better to be sure than sorry. Much packing of clothes, and ironing of jockey colours, and neglecting of school lessons. The blacks are all smiles, and all the girls are buying new dresses from the station store, and the boys are vying to ride for the boss, and training for the foot-races.

The ultimate experience in happiness and good cheer is leaving the station en route for the races. The head-stockman's driving the station truck, with the cowboy-butcher and the book-keeper sitting beside him, and the blacks chattering and cheering on the back, sitting on their swags and yackai-ing to the kids and the governess on the back of the Jeep on top of the swags and the big tuckerbox. Dad's wearing his new hat, and Mum has crammed what Dad calls "the whole darn station" between herself and Dad on the Jeep seat.

Nobody feels the bumps: nobody complains when the truck gets bogged in a sandy creek. All is unity and good cheer, and we all know we've got faster horses, fleeter foot-runners, smarter Aborigines, prettier girls and better fighters than all the other stations and we're out to prove it.

One hundred and fifty happy miles later, and the bush racecourse and the scattered bough-sheds of the stations' camps, the stand, bar and toilets come into view. There's shouting of greetings and chiacking, and our boys are waiting at our camp with the billy on, and the word is the truck with the beer will be here after sundown. (The beer truck never arrives before sundown of the day before the races, even if the driver has to camp half a day on the way. By mutual agreement the padre holds the church service at sundown and performs any requested marriages and christenings, and after the service the ladies produce masterpieces of cakes and pots of tea for supper, while the padre pulls the names out of the hat for the calcutta.

Setting up camp is fairly important; after all you're going to be there for nearly a week. Mum bustles around directing the unloading of cyclone beds for the ladies, tucker boxes, suitcases; Dad checks the champ's training times with the boys, and frowns at reports of the other contenders; the governess is talking to a young ringer from another camp; the Aborigines are setting up their camp with friends and relatives, and eldest son has a grin like a slit in a watermelon and his girl hanging on his arm.

The camp is hectic with comings and goings and conviviality. Mum's up at dawn on the first day of the races setting out breakfast on the bush-built tables and feeding all-comers. Everyone must wash his own plate and pannikin in the large bucket of hot water by the campfire. Everyone's appetite is enormous, and Mum feels she's been cooking steak for hours over the campfire. She begins to envy a nearby station who have brought their cook with them, safe in the knowledge that he is a teetotaller. Lunch is cold beef, boiled potatoes and tomatoes, so that's easy enough, but she'll have to start early on the stew for supper.

Everyone has gone back to the race-course after lunch, and she's peeling the vegetables, and feeling a bit neglected. Dad's off with his cronies making bets. He comes back to the camp, and she mentions maybe he could enter her on Pieface for the Ladies Race later this afternoon. Dad's not quite sober, and he bellows with laughter and says "Come off it, old girl. Sure-shot Lil's a cert to win that; you'd only make a fool of yourself. You stick to the spuds, that's your game."

Silly, silly man! He goes off, and Mum's lips go thin and her eyes narrow. It's a man's world, is it! Grogging on and never a care in the world while she slaves over a hot campfire. She hasn't the faintest notion how epsom salts got into the tuckerbox — probably the bottle for some horse ailment — but it's the work of a moment to divide the stew into two pans and upend the bottle into the larger pan for the men.

After supper Mum's barely got the kids bedded down and is making her preparations for the dance when Dad and the boys and the ringers start looking uncomfortable.

By the time she's got her sapphire-blue evening frock and her silver evening slippers on, the exodus has started. She doesn't even feel guilty when Dad says "fraid you'll have to go to the dance by yourself dear, I don't feel so hot!" as he dashes past.

The dance floor is a concrete slab with lighting supplied by cars and trucks lined up at intervals with their headlights on. The band consists of two ringers with guitars and a drover with a piano accordion. Mum has a whale of a time.

Mum's popularity goes to her head; she doesn't miss a dance; she feels sixteen again. When she glances over towards the camp she notices the torches flashing to and fro like a bunch of syncopated fireflies.

Mum does enjoy the exhibition Lil puts on, and the cheers rise to the starry heavens, when Lil does the Cossack Dance in the middle of the dance floor before passing out cold and being carried off by son and daughter. She's still giggling when old Cec breathes down her neck and asks her for a dance.

She starts to get apprehensive when they're only half way round the dance floor; who'd have thought the old goat would have so much spark in him. She's jammed up against his hairy chest, and he's snorting like a scrub bull. By the second turn around the floor it's obvious he's planning on one crowded hour of glorious life. His high-heeled boots are stamping out the rhythm and there's an unholy gleam in his beady little eyes.

He's got a grasp on Mum like she's a monkey strap on an outlaw, and the lecherous old brute's steering her off the floor towards his truck, where he says he's got a little bottle of something hidden in the toolbox and his swag's on the back — heh heh!

Despite her frantic protests she's towed off to his truck, but he lets go of her to open his toolbox and she hitches up her sapphire blue and makes a bolt for it. But his blood is up now, and he's not going to be thwarted so easily, "Hoy!" he bellows and thunders after her. She can't run fast in the darn silver slippers, and there's a handy patch of scrub, so she darts into the bushes and pulls them off as he blunders past. But he can't see her ahead, so he stops and back-pedals, all the time pleading in a falsetto bleat for her to be a good sport and have a little drinkie-winkie with Cec.

He's a determined old coot. He flushes her out, and pants after her, waving the bottle. She dodges him behind trees and other people's Jeeps and blitz-buggies, and he's smart enough to cut off her retreat to her own camp — not that there's likely to be much help there! She can't dive for safety onto the lit-up dance floor because a branch has ripped the sapphire blue immodestly, and with old Cec tally -hoing in full pursuit behind her people are going to draw the wrong conclusions.

It takes her half an hour before she finally eludes him and staggers back to the camp, tattered and barefoot.

In the morning Dad and the boys have recovered, and Dad unsuspectingly comments that the meat must have been a bit off in the big stew. They're happy again, keen to make up for lost time, Mum's reprieved.

In the camp on the other side of the river Lil's meek daughter is explaining that the only medicine for a hangover is called hair-of-the-dog, and is administering straight vodka to her mother on the suggestion of the only boyfriend she's ever been able to acquire because her mother was out of the way.

The champ wins the Cup, and the elder son's girl is all smiles because he's won the Bracelet for her on the mare. Toby's second in the Aborigines' Race, and Long Maggie flies home in the lubras' footrace. The kids find a pound note and nobody claims it so they take it to the bookie and bet on the champ in the Cup. And the cooking is great; Mum works like a beaver, all smiles too. It's a great meeting — equally as good as last year's.

Help stamp out
mail order

Help stamp our mail order

One of the pleasures that townsfolk never know is that of opening a mail-order parcel and finding the contents to be exactly what you ordered from the catalogue, or at least a reasonable substitute.

It doesn't happen very often, due to a combination of transceiver static, postal strikes, and half-witted shop assistants.

Given the odds against remote-order satisfaction, it is fair to assume that one parcel in ten will be satisfactory, and it is my theory, based on thirty years' observations, that the colourful language of the far outback bears no relation to the hardships of the early bullockies, but rather has evolved from the frustrations of remote order consignees.

I urgently needed a small suitcase for an unexpected flying visit where the well-groomed sophisticate was the impression I wished to make. The static was bad when I sent my telegram, but I didn't expect to receive a small fruitcake in the mail, and my best bib-and-tucker carried in a patched mailbag did nothing for my sophisticate image.

I forget what it was we'd ordered when we received the huge cement-mixer from our agents on Xmas Eve. There was just time to send them a telegram — "thanks for Xmas present stop would have preferred cash as already have cement-mixer." That stimulated a bit of agent activity, and the poor fellow waiting urgently on his cement-mixer got it for the New Year.

When Joe bought the first tractor for our NT station it was a gala day, and we all cheered as the ponderous machine was manoeuvred off the truck. In between swatting inquisitive kids the boss established that the operator's manual was missing, there was no tool kit, and the rev. counter gauge didn't work. The tractor looked impressive, but it didn't go.

This being the golden sixties, the agent chartered a plane and brought out a mechanic, complete with tools and the missing manual, and after smoko they all adjourned to the shed.

"These little things happen, Joe. We'll soon have her right," said the agent, as he opened the manual with a flourish and ran his finger down the index. "Here we are, page 18." Pages 16 to 24 were completely blank. At regular intervals through the two-inch thick manual eight blank pages greeted the enraged eyes of the bewildered agent. "These little things happen," commented Joe wearily, "but about having her right, it depends on what you mean by soon!" (Naturally, the tools replaced by the manufacturers belonged to a different model.)

I remember with a shudder my attempts to order a lollabout. At the time the catalogues and women's magazines figured lollabouts on every second page. There were ladies luxuriating on lollabouts beside swimming pools, on patios, on green acres of lawn in front of magnificent mansions. Nothing would satisfy me but that I must have a lollabout for Xmas, so we set the wheels in motion with a telegram to the agents.

The transport arrived, and I'll swear they must have had to leave half the loading behind to fit the monstrosity aboard. Where the agents resurrected it from must for ever remain a mystery; the only place it could conceivably have been appropriate was on an elephant's back in the retinue of a particularly opulent rajah at the turn of the century. It was green and gold, and fringed and curtained and be-ribboned, and large enough to accommodate the questionable going-ons of two rajahs and half-a-dozen concubines. I was appalled. I flew inside and sent an impassioned telegram — "returning howdah. Send lollabout urgent, " — and rushed out again to disperse the giggling house-girls and speculating ringers.

It's going to strain your credulity; it certainly strained mine. You wouldn't believe there could be two of them extant. The next truck arrived a week before Xmas, and delivered me a blue and pink twin, looped, fringed and curtained as before. (Children, chooks, and black-fellows flew for cover as I delivered my opinion of the merchandise department and the designer who had conceived the unspeakable creation.) When I calmed down the truckie suggested that he took a picture back to town and arranged with the agent to send me a lollabout with the mission truck on Xmas Eve. So we cut a picture out of the catalogue, and everyone comforted me with "Third time lucky, Mum." On Xmas Eve we got the green and gold one back again. The only reason we didn't change agents was that we owed them too much money. The kids made me a lollabout out of an old cyclone bed and some strips of greenhide.

I was luckier than Joe. His telegram was explicit enough, when he ordered chain saw parts by names and part numbers, ending with an 18" bar, part number so and so.

He got a complete new chainsaw, and a jemmy, and a collection of miscellaneous items — we still don't know what they were.

The same week his request for a 24" refrigerator belt netted him a 24" bolt threaded at both ends. If they couldn't do anything else, at least they could measure right.

There seems to be a voodoo on our family regarding cement-mixers: another station, another State, another agent, but the same old story.

Joe inspected the display model mixer on the shop floor, and accepted delivery of the crated model from the storeroom. As we were building yards, taking delivery of cattle, and a host of other jobs, he didn't uncrate it until he was ready to use it. When he went to assemble it, he found a cracked ring and a whole section of parts missing.

With no phone or transceiver, contacting the shop involved me battling through trackless scrub, crossing a river that frightened the wits out of me, and ringing up on a neighbour's party-line. I read the part-numbers from the assembly instructions, and the clerk promised to airfreight them from the manufacturers and send them the following week with some loading. Loading arrived — no parts.

Another trip through the scrub, a different clerk on the phone. He couldn't find any reference to the order — the first clerk had gone on holidays. So I repeated the details and arranged for the parts to be sent to a township fifty miles away. No, of course they weren't there when I called a fortnight later. When I rang up nobody seemed to know what I was talking about.

To make a long story short, three months later I drove 120 long skinny miles to town, absolutely determined that I was going to return with the rest of the cement-mixer we'd paid for way back in June. I had my 13-year-old daughter for a back-up.

We reconnoitred the shop floor. There was the display model, gleaming, complete, all parts operative, — we checked! I was polite; I exuded charm to the sales manager, even when he claimed that he had no knowledge of the 17 or 18 phone calls I'd made. I suggested that he give me the necessary parts from the display model and replace them with the parts he claimed he would air-freight up for me by next week.

But he said he was sorry he couldn't do that; it wasn't really a display model; as a matter of fact he'd sold it two days before, and it was going to be picked up by a client tomorrow. I said, "Oh, what a shame," winked at my daughter, and asked him to show me some welders which were on display around the corner of the L-shaped showroom.

I asked him fatuous questions for ten minutes, stretched the conversation a little longer by checking all the parts — was he sure, ha ha, that the crated ones would be complete? He was beginning to get a little terse with me by the time daughter turned up and reminded me of a fictitious appointment.

We were elated; she's a handy kid with a spanner, and she'd removed the whole section neatly, and there it was on the Toyota seat between us.

We drove home gleefully, happy in the knowledge that we'd done our bit for the family honour, and just on sundown we pulled up in front of the shed, and bore the missing parts in triumph to the boss.

To the female eye all these parts look alike when they are only described to you; we'd pinched the wrong section. However, it did give me a bargaining advantage. Once more across the river to the phone, and I made it quite clear to the sales manager that I wouldn't give him back these parts till he got me the right ones, and I didn't care what his other client was saying, and what's more he'd have to organise getting the parts out to us, and while he was still spluttering I hung up on him.

Six days later we had the parts, but the whole exercise had taken six months.

Every farmer and every grazier has experiences like this, but very occasionally some grazier does have a win. Our partner in the Kimberleys arranged transport from Adelaide for a station stallion at the same time as a Territory man organised transport with the same agents for an unseen race-horse.

Gee, our partner's buck threw some fleet-footed foals by the station mares before the Territory man realised that seven lasts in the Darwin races weren't due to climatic changes and new surroundings.

Kimberley
and rasp

champagne
berry jam

R. Wanis.

Melissa was ratting around in the medical chest. She came up with an aah of satisfaction and a plastic syringe.

"Somebody hurt?" I enquired mildly.

"Nope. I just want to ice the Christmas cake, and we haven't got an icing set".

Well, why would we need one? Mandy iced the cake last year, and wrote "Merry Xmas, Mob" with the aid of a white-shoe cleaner tube. She cut the bottom out of the tube, squeezed the cleaner into a jar, washed the tube out and filled it with icing.

The neat little slash she made in the silver seal at the top was just right for the writing, and when she made a second cut at right angles it produced excellent rosettes.

You need to be able to make substitutions in the bush, or you might as well be living in the suburbs.

I don't mean you have to go the whole hog and indulge in Kimberley Champagne — metho and Sal Vital — but there are occasions when more than the luxuries of life are dependent on an effective substitute.

It's quite a few years now since Kurt Johannsen crash-landed his little plane on a clay-pan in central Australia and snapped the propeller. He might not have got out of that alive if he hadn't been able to carve himself a new prop out of mulga wood to replace the broken one, and fly himself back to Alice Springs.

Getting yourself out of a breakdown situation is probably the best impetus for finding a satisfactory substitute from limited resources.

I recall the days when the ubiquitous marmite jar was more often doing service as a filter than reposing in the tucker box.

Mulga can be used for a variety of motor repairs too. You can Cobb and Co a mulga branch to the spring if you're got a broken mainleaf; a splinter carefully shaved does duty as the needle for a needle and seat; and after two or three tries you can carve a rotor arm if there is no other way of getting one.

But probably the most important resource for the bush traveller is number 8 fencing wire. A pair of 12" pliers, some wire and a Cobb and Co hitch have been the means of bringing more journeys to a successful conclusion than promises broken by politicians.

It's not three months since I used a length of number 8 wire for a tow rope, and Sammy was only seven the first time he wired my exhaust back on with good old number 8.

You can join most parts of a vehicle together with it; for building repairs it has few equals; and in the days before Hills Hoists everyone who didn't have a creek and a flat rock handy used it for a clothes line. (However, I don't know that I actually approve of the technique of a male friend of mine, who substituted barbed wire for number 8 so he wouldn't have to use pegs.)

Before his days of wedded bliss, someone I know fairly well, never noted for his sartorial elegance, actually used tie-wire to mend rents in his trousers, but nowadays Mandy is fairly handy with the needle and less able to ignore the insistent demands of the mending basket than either Melissa or I.

The tuckerbox can supply more than marmite jars in times of necessity. Powdered milk for a hole in the radiator, soap for a hole in the petrol tank, black sauce for a lubricant and Joe likes raspberry jam for a substitute belt-dressing. He keeps the plum jam for when he's out of sugar.

And if you want to know why so many bush wives appear in town bare-legged it's because their husbands have borrowed their pantyhose on the way in to town as a stand-in for a broken fan belt.

Yes, of course most wives own more than one pair, but if you camp overnight and Pete trades the rope tying down the load with a passing Aborigine for three malodorous dingo-scalps you don't have much chance of retaining the four pairs in your suitcase when the necessity is explained to you. You can belt Pete when you get home, and confiscate his dingo-scalps, but there's no store handy to trade the scalps for new pantyhose.

There comes the occasion when no amount of fencing wire, mulga wood, or powdered milk will suffice. If it's tyre trouble, three wrecked tubes and a hundred miles to go, you have to pack the tyres with spinifex.

This can be rough on delicate hands — unless you've got the kids with you — and it's a bumpy ride, but you take it steady, it saves the rims and gets you a nod of approval from the boss when you finally jolt in to the station yard.

I was always careful to carry plenty of spare oil, so I never had to try packing the diff with white ants, and I wouldn't like to try it these days for fear of bringing down the wrath of the animal libbers on my head.

Frankie claims there are travellers on bush roads these days who don't know what to do when they've got a puncture and lost their jack. I find that hard to believe, but Mandy assures me that it's only a few weeks since she had to show a city family how to jam a rock under the vehicle to hold it and dig a hole under the wheel.

Pete said why didn't she lend them her jack, but Mandy said she had a civic duty to show them in case they got another puncture further on and perished themselves just because she had taken the easy way out; and she was not just showing off, so there!

Back at the homestead, it's not fair to blame Mum for not thinking ahead and preparing for special occasions, if she has a tribe of kids who smell out, track down, and steal without conscience such goodies as she may have cached against the festivities.

Chocolate-starved fathers sometimes have no more conscience than their offspring. Such mothers are often obliged to substitute.

Melissa, at six, came stamping into the kitchen on Easter Sunday.

"That rotten Easter Bunny!" she expostulated. It wasn't the boiled eggs with faces painted on them which annoyed her; it was the trite little note informing her that boiled eggs were better for her teeth than chocolate ones. Well, you live and learn.

I've got a quick ginger beer recipe for use when the last of the Christmas lolly-water runs out two days before Christmas. You mix three pounds of sugar and four tablespoons of ground ginger, four dessertspoons of cream of tartar, four teaspoons of tartaric acid, and a cup of yeast, in four gallons of water, stand four hours, and bottle.

I ought to explain that a cup of yeast means one heaped teaspoon of yeast made up in a cup of water. The first time a neighbour used my recipe and emptied a full cup of Dribarm into the brew the potency of the result played havoc on the unsuspecting consumer.

Some passing ringers were invited to partake when the batch was broached, and four gallons and three days later the station began to return to normality. As a competitor to Kimberley Champagne it had a slight edge because the recovery rate was quicker. (The original recipe, I emphasise, is quite suitable for children and visiting teetotallers.)

The Early Days

Planning is hardly worthwhile

When I first went north to Hall's Creek I thought I may as well have a look at the N.T. before I went south again, so I applied for a job in the store at Victoria River Downs. Getting from Halls Creek to V.R.D. was supposedly simple — there was an outback plane service — so I paid ten pounds for the fare and climbed into the Dragon Rapide with my swag and suitcase.

That trip is probably a fair example of how the seemingly simple things you have to do in the outback never seem to go according to plan. On paper all I had to do was get in the plane, admire the scenery as we flew east, and four hours later, after landing and taking off at a few stations on the way, I should have stepped out on the V.R.D. airstrip.

The trip actually took ten days. We were hardly in the air when a call came on the radio to make a deviation to a station 100 miles west of Halls Creek. I was the only passenger, and by the time we landed there I was so airsick that I'd thrown up all over the mail-bags and nothing was going to get me back into that little plane. Eddie Connellan couldn't have agreed with me more. He gave me back my ten pounds and borrowed a bucket and mop to clean up his plane.

That left me 100 miles further west than when I'd started. I stayed there two days. On Day 3 I was escorted on a borrowed horse, with my gear on a packhorse, across the range to another station whose owner drove me back to Halls Creek on Day 4.

Days 5 and 6 were spent on, off, and under a truck which broke down twenty-three times before it crossed the border to Nicholson Station. Once there it rained — too wet to nurse that unspeakable truck any further — so there I stayed until Day 8, when the mailplane arrived. The plane had already been to V.R.D. — it always came from V.R.D. to Nicholson, so my only recourse was to go north-west instead of south-east. Therefore, suitably doped on airsickness tablets, I flew to Wyndham.

Wyndham is hot and humid, and I struck its hottest, most humid day during the era when a punkah was considered the very latest thing in air-conditioning. I dripped through Day 9 and flew to V.R.D. on Day 10. I didn't know if I still had the job, and by that time I wasn't madly impressed with our far North. Rusty, the pilot, offered the opinion that I'd be like all the other girls he ferried out to V.R.D. "You'll marry a ringer and end up in a boundary-rider's hut," he said.

I smartly bet him ten quid that no such fate awaited me.

Well, I've never seen Rusty since, but I consider that I only owe him five quid, because our shed is a lot bigger than a boundary-rider's hut, and Joe does a lot of other things besides riding our boundaries.

When Robbie Burns wrote about best-laid plans aft ganging agley, little did he know how much further agley the plans of outback Australians could gang than those of mere Scottish mice and men. I knew a reputable gentleman from the Fitzroy River who planned every year for twenty years to spend Christmas in Perth. He usually got as far as Derby, arriving there on the eve of the day the Koolinda was due to dock. Late boats, rotten poker hands, dog-eating crocodiles, and the second World War — one or the other, or a combination, all contrived so that he never did make a landfall at Fremantle.

It didn't take me long to realise that the duration of a journey, by whatever means of transport, might depend on the weather, the availability of spare parts, the number of hospitable people you met on the way, or any of a dozen barely-credible reasons. Joe's instruction to me not to come looking for him until he was two days overdue was standard instruction to bush wives. The advent of portable transceivers didn't mean that the journeys were achieved in the planned time, but at least you then knew why the travellers were delayed.

The town-dwellers weren't much better off than the bushies when it came to making long-range plans. The wedding date of a young couple in Alice Springs had been set for three months. They were wed in the church on the Town side of the Todd River and the reception was to be held on the East side. It rained up in the hills and the Todd came down in a flash flood. Only a trickle at first so the bridal party and most of the guests got across. The groom and best man then drove back to ferry the last of the guests over before the water rose too high. Guess who spent his wedding night on Town side while the bride and guests went ahead with the reception on East side?

Our own wedding was more of a spontaneous affair (the result of a series of apparently unconnected circumstances which all the planning in the world couldn't have bettered). Bushies from various outposts had gathered in Katherine for a race-meeting; my governess sister was in town; the hawker's van had an unexpected white dress among the sensible coloured prints on the shelves; a Salvation Army padre worked in town; and Joe gave me the ultimatum "Marry me today — or not at all!"

Some instinct told me he meant it, and seeing it was delivered to me shouted across the road outside the pub while he brandished a four-foot stuffed crocodile at me for emphasis, it wasn't surprising that the spectators soon became involved.

There was general consensus that he was a good bloke. Then someone wanted to know if I could cook. So I said yes before he found out I couldn't. That was 11 a.m. We were married by the padre at 7 p.m. A friend cut down the hawker's-van dress to fit me and lent us her wedding ring. My sister was bridesmaid. Her boss organised the wedding breakfast, and his wife reduced Joe's outback-ringer hairstyle to bridegroom proportions. I don't know who iced two fruit cakes from the store for a two-tier wedding cake, or who stole the bouquet from the only rose-garden in town, but it was the publican who offered the pub for the reception, and a passing grader-driver who took the wedding photos. All our outback friends were there, including some late-comers in a transport and a utility who were passing through Katherine en route to Darwin.

We got our first set of flat-sided billycans among the wedding presents. They came in handy later when Joe taught me to cook.

If I'm suffering why
shouldn't others suffer!

Are there any farm wives who feel guilty when they read magazine stories about the brave little women carrying on with a smile in the teeth of adversity; bearing the brunt of the family misfortunes; and selflessly "going without" to make things a lot easier for the family? Well, if you must read that sort of stuff, serves you right. If the going is crook, you've got every right to whinge and snarl periodically, just like everyone else does. Moreover, a good burst of bad behaviour gets all the resentment out of your system, and you can be genuinely pleasant and unselfish for a while to make up for it: consistently unselfish wives and mothers get taken for granted.

I was a thoroughly selfish little brat as a child and my godmother apparently thought to alter this unpleasant trait by presenting me with a story book relating the adventures of a dear little girl called Pollyanna, who didn't have much going for her. I remember she was permanently on crutches, and I think she was an orphan. Despite these handicaps she influenced all with whom she came in contact, by playing "The Glad Game". Pollyanna always found something to be glad about, never once indulging in legitimate grumbles over the dirty deals Fate handed her with amazing frequency. This uncharacteristic behaviour influenced and eventually won over even the most fiendishly selfish children in her orbit.

For the first few chapters I was impressed, and almost on the point of considering a local version of the Glad game. Halfway through the book I became increasingly irritated by Pollyanna's goody-goody exploits, and by the end I had totally rejected the ghastly little prig and her stupid game. Just one naughty tantrum to make her human like me, and I might have swallowed the bait, but overdoing the message resulted in an immediate return to my childhood philosophy of "If someone hits you, hit `em back, or, if the occasion warrants, hit `em first !"

My reactions to adverse situations mellowed with adolescence, but people in my immediate vicinity were still left in no doubt when I considered that the world had treated me unfairly. Equally, they knew when I had won a round. I saw no point whatsoever in turning the other cheek: doormat behaviour invited being walked over. If Pollyanna could take that, while feeling glad the wearer was barefooted instead of wearing bob-nailed boots, that was her look-out; I didn't buy that attitude at all.

I haven't changed my philosophy much, but I have outgrown one of its nastier side-effects — the "if I'm suffering why shouldn't others suffer" syndrome. The momentary feeling of satisfaction isn't worth the ensuing feeling of shame. I'm able to report that I have actually reversed that unpleasant trait, so that I can now honestly say "good luck to them" without a trace of resentment when somebody achieves a goal which I can't attain.

The change dates from the first winter of our marriage, which sneaked up on us in an isolated settlement ill-supplied with furniture and the necessities of life, and 700 miles from the nearest point of purchase of same. We had to make-do with what we had.

The marriage bed was two cyclone wire-stretchers pushed together, thin horsehair mattresses, and two thin grey Army blankets. This arrangement had served quite adequately during the summer months, but then came the first cold snap. This onslaught of winter coincided with a visit by a friend of my parents, who was being treated to a non-stop exhibition of marital bliss, so she would take the right report home to the suburbs.

Our bed was on the east verandah, hers was on the west. That night, a cold, clear moon shone down on the peaceful homestead, where two of its three inhabitants were dreaming happily. I couldn't even doze, I was so cold, and my feet grew icier by the minute. What more natural than to snuggle over to my loving husband and put my cold feet on the back of his legs to warm them up. That was when I discovered for the first time that he is not at his best when woken suddenly from a sound sleep. Instead of comfort I got a muted snarl. Then he moved over and went straight back to sleep.

The thermometer dropped another ten degrees. I crept over to his warm bulk and burrowed close. He didn't wake but he moved away. That took the warmth away, so I followed. He moved again — I followed. One more move and he fell off the edge of the bed.

With a not-so-muted snarl this time, he picked himself up, padded down the verandah to his swag, hauled it out on the lawn, unrolled it, climbed in, and immediately slept. Without him there, the bed was now a complete ice-box. There was no chance of sleep for me. I was tired, I was bitterly cold, and that

made me mean as well. And I got meaner with every freezing minute.

"If I'm cold," I reasoned, "why shouldn't he be!"

"We share for better or worse" I recalled. "Well, we're going to share this worse bit !"

I got up, sneaked to the kitchen, and got a jug of iced water from the fridge. I tip-toed out onto the lawn, stared for a long moment at the sleeping hump in the moon-light, then suddenly snatched back his blankets and chucked the whole jugful of icy water over the inconsiderate brute.

He came up out of the swag like a banshee, making choking spluttering noises of such implicit menace that I didn't stop to argue. I went for my life round the end of the house dropping the jug as I ran. He came after me like an arrow. But even in our extremity we were both aware of our visitor's presence and no sound other than hard panting passed our lips. I'd been a long-distance runner, and I was still fit, which was probably just as well, because he didn't look like catching me for the first three circuits of the house, and it took that distance for his murderous intent to dissipate, and his sense of the ridiculous to surface. We collapsed giggling on the lawn. All was well. He had to come back to the bed because his swag was wringing wet, and my impromptu run had warmed me up.

Our friend commented at breakfast that she'd thoroughly enjoyed the nocturnal entertainment after our sickeningly amorous behaviour since her arrival, and as we'd flashed past her verandah on each successive round of the house, she'd almost been moved to sit up and cheer.

I had the grace to feel slightly ashamed of myself, but what really cured me was the realisation of what might have happened if he'd caught me in the first ten yards. There's always the chance that if you make someone suffer just because you're suffering, you might end up suffering more than you bargained for.

So, while I don't recommend the "brave little woman in adversity" type, it's not a bad idea to mix a little bit of the Pollyanna in with the grumbles, just to keep the status quo.

Six goannas plus five goannas equals big mob

Some are born teachers; some are made teachers; and some have teaching thrust upon them — as many an outback mother will corroborate. It was thrust upon me when a dozen or so naked piccaninnies, led by a sophisticated ten-year-old in shorts, accosted me. As their spokesman, and the only one who could speak English, the trousered young man put their case.

"What about school, Missus!"

Lindsay had recently arrived from a Settlement Mission Station, and was a fount of knowledge on the amenities of the outside world. I suspect his credibility had been questioned by the deposed leaders of the gang, and that he was appealing to me to support him as to the existence of such things, rather than from any real desire to have his freedom curtailed in the pursuit of knowledge.

However, it seemed a good idea, especially to Joe, who could easily do without the daily pranks of a marauding band of "pics", led by an imaginative and enterprising young general. So we swung into action.

Joe cleaned out the old store-room for the school-house, and made two long trestle tables and forms from planks. He improvised a blackboard and tacked it to the wall, and the pics helped to paint it. The lean-to beside the schoolhouse was the bath-house, with two forty-four gallon drums cut lengthwise to make four tubs, and the water-supply was a third upright drum refilled every morning, with a bucket beside it to dip out the water or to heave water over an unsuspecting comrade when the Missus wasn't looking. The first half-hour of the school day was devoted to bathing and dressing in "school clothes". What a delightful riot that was!

I had an off-sider named Millie, whose job it was to supervise bath-time, clothes issue, and hair-combing, while I hurriedly learned the Aboriginal words from my house-girls for the English equivalents I intended to impart that day.

Our school was a real community effort. Millie usually had an offsider or two of her own to help with the morning ablutions and the washing of school clothes and towels when we reclaimed them at the end of the day's lessons. A couple of mothers and hangers-on were co-opted to cook a mid-day meal for the pics; the stock-camp gave us a condamine bell; two of the old men of the tribe paid us regular inspectorial visits; and a father representing the P. & C. presented me with a specially-made nulla-nulla in case any of my pupils showed signs of "too much cheeky-bugger" behaviour.

The whole tribe, as well as Joe, obviously considered it a jolly good thing to have the pics pinned-down and out of mischief for a good part of the day, and they weren't about to see the idea fall through if they could prevent it. A letter to the Education Department in Darwin garnered a crate of pads, pencils, coloured chalks and paints, and a graded set of reading books specially written for Aboriginal children, which were great as the children began to learn simple English sentences. The pics put the same enthusiasm into their schooling as they had into their mischief, and I had to keep the condamine bell in my bedroom overnight for the first few weeks, or someone would be likely to steal it and ring it for school at any time from 5 a.m. onwards.

In view of my later career I realise that no teacher ever had it so good; those pics were the keenest students I ever had. It wasn't an official school, and there wasn't a salary, but they did learn something, and so did I. I learned a basic truth. They didn't have to attend school, and I didn't have to teach them; we did it because we chose to, and because it was voluntary we enjoyed it.

As in all schools parents were sometimes a problem. I had to make sure that the sons of two competitive brothers achieved equally, or the lagging offspring was likely to get a back-hander from Dad. And there was quite a complicated tribal argument as to whether the girls would be allowed to attend — eight-year-old "promised" wives had to have their future husbands' permission — but I got around that by including sewing in the curriculum and hinting no girls — no school. The doubters came round when the tribal big-shot announced his preference for a "proper-smart" number four wife.

Lindsay was my star pupil. He led the singing; he relayed the instructions; he organised the sports. He knew the ropes from previous experience, and I came to depend on him. So when he did not appear one morning I asked if he was sick. No-one would comment. I was mystified, because suddenly it seemed as if he had never existed — adults and children alike just stared blankly at me. Joe explained to me at smoko that Lindsay had been "promoted". By tribal law he was now of an age to be made man, and his education was now in the hands of his tribal uncles. Among other things, this included a six months' ban of silence except for the daily recitation of tribal songs and lore, and a thousand-mile trek along all the "dreaming" paths of the Wailbri history. His name could not be spoken until he returned six months later, a proven young man. There was, of course, no possibility of his return to school, and in twos and threes the boys, as they approached twelve or thirteen, would silently disappear from the ranks.

The girls, from the age of eight, lived in the camps of their promised husbands to be trained in housewifery by the older wives. Any signs of vanity and pretty hair-ribbons, and you could be sure the senior wives would decide that the husband's supply of hair string was running low, and the girls would appear at school cropped almost bald, having spent the previous evening rolling their shorn locks backwards and forwards on one knee to make them into string.

I had to tailor my lessons to the future prospects of my pupils which, if they were female, were not exactly career-oriented, and whatever I felt privately on the matter, I had to restrain my natural objections to extreme male chauvinism, and act with diplomacy. The little girls were the chattels of their middle-aged husbands, who held complete power over them, and could (and did, even in the Government schools in the '70s — possibly still do) withhold their permission for the girls to attend school.

I taught them basic English and basic arithmetic, and we traded legends and stories. They were natural actors once their shyness was overcome, and wonderful mimics. Our "drama" classes were a vehicle for relating many a station incident, and I never had to guess who the youngsters were imitating: every gesture and expression was exact.

They excelled in singing and drawing, and their powers of observation were astoundingly advanced over white children I later taught. I tried the game of putting a dozen items on a tray, leaving it for a minute, and then removing it and asking the children to draw what they had seen. With hardly more than a glance at the tray even the smallest child would reproduce, not only the full number of items, but even the minutest details, such as perfectly spelt words on books or matchboxes, with colours and dimensions correct. I realised with awe that I couldn't compete with them under similar conditions.

And when we had nature walks I became the pupil, and they were very kind about my mistakes.

My simple hygiene lessons about germs became inextricably related to baby kadaitcha, "you can't see him, but he kill you", and we had a spate of hand-washing for days. Joe's magnifying-glass was a huge success in inspecting ants and grass-hoppers, and a photograph was sheer magic. We didn't have many "resources", but we had plenty of enthusiasm. I wish I could get the same reactions from some of the blasé kids I teach today.

A round or two
with a reptile

It's a great pity that you can't do something for the second time before you have to do it for the first time. What I'm getting at is that if you had the experience up your sleeve you could avoid all those embarrassing situations which result when you dive into the fray fortified by nothing stronger than theory. Instruction manuals, buckets of oral instruction and advice, word-perfect in theory — it counts for absolutely nothing when you are faced with the stark reality of having to actually do something for the first time. (I got 97 percent in a written exam on the Principles of Flight, but I wouldn't even go up in an aeroplane with myself as pilot, let alone expect anyone else to!)

I've lost count now of the number of times I've ejected a snake from a dwelling, but I'm not likely to forget the first time I tried, and even if I was, I can rely on someone in the family to relate the incident with relish any time I'm set to accept the congratulations of female city visitors from whose bedrooms or bathrooms I have just removed an unwelcome serpent.

We'd only been a week at Mongrel Downs, and the warning "bad snake country" was uppermost in my mind. The homestead wasn't quite finished, and there were still tea-chests and cartons to be unpacked. The men had gone mustering, leaving my offsider Lorna, myself, and five small children between us, to hold the fort and get on with the unpacking.

Having regard for the priorities, I had four little desks set up on the verandah, and four little kids with their heads down wrestling with Dick and Dora and Co. Lorna, with little Pete tagging along, was unpacking sheets and towels at the bathroom end of the verandah.

Suddenly, and with the full approval of the reluctant students, our lesson was

interrupted by a shriek of "Missus, Missus, sennake! Bigfella sennake!" I dropped my book and rushed down the verandah. About two feet of long sinister black tail was hanging down nonchalantly from the rafter where the unsealed verandah roof met the partly-finished house ceiling. God knows how much more snake was up there in the ceiling.

My first impulse was to snatch up some provisions and herd the whole family outside, and wait there for three or four days until the men came home to rescue us. But then I remembered the criss-crossing of snake-tracks in the red dust outside the house!

On occasions like this someone must take the lead. "L-l-lorna," I said, "t-t-take the children up the other end of the verandah, and fetch me the boss's gun from the office."

"You'll miss 'im, Mum," remarked five-year-old Mandy, "an' you'll blow a hole in the roof!"

Actually, that possibility had already occurred to me, but I had already considered it as the lesser of two evils. I'd had a vaguely similar experience some years before — another first, you might say — which I'd mucked-up in my own inimitable fashion. We'd been croc-shooting from a little tin boat one night on the Victoria River — only fish crocs, but to a raw newchum the pairs of red eyes on the banks gleaming in our torchlight was more than a little exciting. When one of the boys shot one, and amid splashing and shouting the fools managed to heave it into the boat, I wasn't at all sure that I wanted to participate any further in the experiment. The saurian was about five feet long, and the boat wasn't more than six or seven, and there were already four humans in it. They'd given me the gun to hold.

Well, what would you do if the corpse's tail suddenly started thrashing around and nearly knocked you in the river, and you had a gun in your hand? All right, you'd keep calm and help wrestle the struggling creature overboard. Well, I didn't. I pulled the trigger, missed the croc and shot a hole in the bottom of the boat.

The croc jumped overboard of its own volition, the three boys all screamed words I'd never heard before, and the water started to spurt through the hole. I couldn't see it because someone had dropped the torch, but I could feel it round my ankles. Then someone pulled off his shirt and stuffed it in the hole, and we got to shore just as the boat sank.

Anyway, that case was different. A hole up in a roof on firm land is not nearly so devastating as a hole down in the bottom of a boat in midstream. Lorna handed me the gun, I remembered a box of shells on the dressing table among all the clutter dumped on it in the days before female occupancy, which I hadn't yet cleaned up, and I darted in and grabbed a shell. I'd only need one because I had to get it first shot. Lorna already had the axe handy for me to finish off the job when the snake fell down onto the wooden floor. (I really was going to burr up my new house, wasn't I, but the female protecting her young is capable of extra-ordinary sacrifices.)

I was quite confident I was going to hit it. Steely calm, I inserted the shell.

"Stand well back, everyone!" I ordered, without a quaver in my voice.

With the utmost care and the steadiest of hands I sighted on the exact spot where the snake's body disappeared into the dark interior. And squeezed the trigger. Nothing happened. Anti-climax. I sighted again, and once more slowly and firmly squeezed the trigger. Still nothing. The proposed victim must now have sensed some of the tense atmosphere.

Above us the tail twitched, withdrew an inch, flicked sideways. With mouths open we watched as a five-toed foot appeared, and with a heave and a twist four feet of rough-tail goanna backed out of the ceiling and ambled off along the rafter to seek out a quieter haven for a nap.

When Joe got home I told him his gun was no good, and if I was going to be left alone at the homestead and expected to protect his offspring from all exigencies, then I felt I should be provided with something a little more reliable than that old thing.

"What old thing?" he said curiously.

I produced it from the office, warning him that, contrary to his instructions, it still had the bullet in it, because I didn't know how to get it out. He removed the bullet, examined it closely, and his lips began to twitch, and he said in a kindly voice, "Honey, this gun is a .310. But this shell is a .22." He laid the gun on the table. "It's just as well that it didn't go off, because it might have shattered the barrel."

Smart-alec Sammy was inspecting the gun. "No worry — bullet couldn't get out, Dad! There's a hornet's nest right up the barrel!" Even Lorna laughed at me, and she should have been on my side; two of the kids were hers.

So when someone says "Remember the time Mum shot the snake" they are really talking about the time I didn't shoot the goanna.

Three tons of sugar, please

My first experience with an outback store was in the Kimberleys, where all goods changed hands for gold-dust or redolent dingo-scalps. There were pennyweight scales on the counter to weigh the gold in lieu of a till, and smelly sugar-bags of scalps in a pile behind the counter. My second was in Western Queensland, where they gave you your change in shin-plasters; and the third was on a large Northern Territory station where I took a job.

There were a number of outstations and a large staff, both black and white, and we sold everything a bushman could need from saddles, swag covers, and rations to clothing and hair-combs. Actual money didn't figure here either: the employees booked up their purchases in the docket book and, once a month, the total was entered in the debit columns of their accounts. When they went on holidays or pulled out they got a cheque. It was a good way of saving.

I was neither experienced in store-keeping nor as yet fluent in the language of the outback, and my first customer was a tall, grinning Aboriginal ringer who told me his name was Belinda and he wanted "chented chope 'n chirrup". A frantic appeal to the second customer, the overseer, finally resulted in my finding Splinter's name in the docket book and charging up bath soap and golden syrup.

I wasn't too adept in the hardware department either; I thought the customer who asked for a bastard file was being vulgar, and I took lucky dips for pliers, fencing, ordinary, or electricians.

But after a time I did learn the various items and their uses, as well as a certain amount of local knowledge, such as that there would likely be a rush on aspirin and stomach powders shortly after I'd filled an order for "dried apricots, metholated spirits and yeast, and if you're out of apricots make it a couple of pounds of raisins and a bottle of lemon essence".

Soon I could cope with most customers, but I wasn't able to satisfy the request of one who, with a history of periodic bouts of violent insanity, scowled his way in one morning and demanded "a new head — this one's no damn good!" We didn't carry the item, I explained.

"Well, give me an axe then!" he snarled. Obviously he intended to get a head for himself if I wouldn't sell him one.

"Just a moment," I faltered, "the axes are out the back." And so was I. Fast.

"Syrup" was always a mainstay in the outback stores. Joe took over a manager's job once from an old bachelor who wasn't too keen on the silvertail job of office work, and preferred to devote his time to the stock-camp. No time for stock-taking, so year after year he just copied out the preceding year's order and posted it off. When Joe arrived, he investigated the store and, in unopened crates and piled high on cobwebby shelves, he found enough blackstrap molasses to pave an airstrip.

On a family station the store is always out of bounds to the younger children, but on occasions they infiltrate, with sometimes devastating results, as a mother of a pair of lively four-year-old twins discovered to her cost. Cereal manufacturers frequently included cards or toys in the inner packet, and in this particular order the toy was a plastic draught-horse with articulated legs, which "walked" when placed on a sloping surface. The bigger kids decided that the horses would be claimed on the oldest first scale, and, although the twins ate double helpings for a couple of days, it was going to take them longer than they cared to wait to get their share.

Mum forgot to lock the store one morning after she'd been in for a packet of mixed fruit. She didn't miss the twins until the cake was in the oven. An instinct whispered "Store!" to her, but she was too late.

Eight cartons of cereal, each containing twenty-four packets, had been broached. The twins had a two-gallon bucket full of plastic horses, and the heap of cereal on the floor was three feet high and six feet across.

Ordering stores for a year is no job for a jackeroo; you need experience to achieve that fine balance between running out of essentials and finding yourself with three tonnes of weevily flour and a tonne of rotten potatoes still on hand. If you run out of rations you just tighten the belt and sit out the Wet until the loading can get through; the privilege of a plane chartered at the tax-payers' expense does not extend to everyone.

The day our loading arrived was second only to Xmas Day. The kids would voluntarily clean out the store in readiness, and there was never any dearth of labour to help manhandle the fifties of flour, seventies of sugar, tea-chests, sides of leather, and cardboard cartons of tinned goods and clothing. Wax matches, ringers' hats, boiled lollies, jam, tinned butter and cheese, brooms, flash shirts, high-heeled boots, tinned fish, dried fruit, mirrors, combs, tools, tinned fruit, tobacco, swag covers, and pocket knives; when they were all finally sorted and installed on their correct shelves the assistants were rewarded with a handful of boiled lollies, and the head-stockman performed his ritual of tearing off the labels from the tinned fruit cans for the stockcamp (because he couldn't stand the arguments on Sundays over whether they'd have peaches, pears, or apricots for sweets.)

Sammy and Mandy would load up a wheelbarrow with goodies to go direct to my pantry, and there would be a gala feast that night, fresh potatoes and onions always voted the most popular items.

` Next day everyone bought a new hat. The head-stockman, hero-worshipped for his prowess and expertise as a horseman, was accorded first choice, and if he chose a black hat it was black hats all round, ringers, kids, goatherds, and all. Pocket-knives came next, at varying prices. They were favoured items to bet with in the card-games after supper in the camp.

I loved the atmosphere and the aromas of the station store with replenished stocks. I suppose it was because the stacked shelves represented security for another year, white-ants and cyclones permitting. (You needn't count unstable dynamite among the hazards because only a real jackeroo would be stupid enough to store the dynamite and detonators in close proximity to twenty-seven fifties of flour and six cartons of golden syrup.)

All I want for Xmas
is the mail

When we lived in the Northern Territory we didn't have a mail service because our area was classified as "tiger country" where only twin-engined planes were supposed to fly, and the local mail-contractor didn't have a twin to spare. Our mail used to stack up in the stock-agent's office in town, dependent on the good offices of truckies, government officials on business bent, and aspiring travellers who called at the office in the hope of getting reliable advice about the condition of the road.

Consequently our magazines were a bit out-of-date when we received them but the advantage was that you could usually read the whole serial in one sitting. You couldn't be sure that the fashions were still trendy, but that was hardly a consideration in the land where jeans, shirt, and elastic sides were more-or-less standard apparel.

The longest spell we had without a mail in or out was twelve weeks, because the February Wet was particularly heavy and closed the road until early May. It was toughest on 13-year-old Melissa, homesick at boarding school in Perth. Although I wrote every week I couldn't post the letters, so she didn't get any mail from home until the last week of term, when twelve letters arrived together, just in time to dissipate her growing conviction that she was really an orphan who'd only imagined that she'd once had a family.

With this erratic type of delivery we were quite innured to stale news and irate letters from creditors who frankly didn't believe my excuses for late payments. (But I'd been broken-in early to city disbelief in country conditions when a suburban post-office official adamantly refused to accept an outpost radio telegram to Joe advising him of Melissa's arrival, on the grounds that there wasn't any such address. My weeping insistence that I lived there too moved him not one whit, and I finally had to take a taxi to the city G.P.O. to send my telegram.)

But the one mail I did like to see arrive on time was the Xmas mail, because it really is anti-climatic to open parcels and read cards in mid-January or maybe even February, and I'm happy to report that a rough check reveals that we got our mail on time about one out of every two Xmases.

It was a near thing one Xmas though. I'd almost resigned myself to the fact that it was going to be one of the off years when, five days before Xmas, the Mission truck from the West called in en route to town. I gave the driver our out-going mail to post and asked him to pick up our in-coming mail and a dozen bars of bread.

When he returned two days before Xmas it was obvious he'd had a traumatic trip. Getting away from town can be difficult any time of year when you have to round up passengers who don't want to leave the fleshpots, but during Xmas week the probability of achieving this aim diminishes meteorically. He had five of the original eight passengers he'd taken to town, which was a pretty good average I thought, but judging by their surly expressions they'd rather have been with the absconders — two in jail and one could be anywhere. He'd collected the bread, but hadn't remembered the mail until he had the complaining passengers on the back of the truck, and he knew that if he stopped again they'd all jump off and disappear and he'd be back where he'd started from early that morning.

I knew from bitter experience what the priorities were, so I accepted his apologies and the two bags of bread — six bars to a bag, packed hot and fresh by the baker, and sat on for 400 miles by one or the other, or the lot, of his rotten passengers. Sammy hauled the squashed mess over to the chook-house and the chooks got a bonus feed.

At first I was sorry for myself and then I got mad. I was going to have the Xmas mail, and I wasn't going to bake bread tomorrow. Maybe an 800-mile round trip wasn't warranted for a few Xmas cards, but it was the bread which clinched my determination.

Joe and the stockcamp were due in on Xmas Eve, but I had one offsider on the station. While he filled-up the car with petrol, checked spares, tucker box, water, I threw instructions to the kids. Melissa and Mandy could cook the chooks and the last-minute goodies, and the boys could get a Xmas tree and put up the decorations, and any boy stealing the nuts or lollies would get a thrashing on my return, Xmas or no Xmas.

It was a twelve-hour drive to town in those days, and a sign sixteen miles north of Alice Springs asserted that the road was suitable for four-wheel-drive vehicles only, but I calculated that by taking the car through the sandy stretches at night, and with two drivers, we ought to be able to do the trip in twenty-four hours.

We left home after tea and made good time, cruising into town just on sun-up. There were two mail-bags, all bulging with parcels and letters; the baker produced fresh warm bars of bread which we carefully stowed in the boot; the fruit shop was just taking delivery of cases of stone-fruit from Adelaide.

I don't think the kids had ever tasted peaches or cherries — we never saw such luxuries in the outback. Gleefully I purchased peaches, apricots, nectarines, the lot! It took an hour to do my extra shopping and another two to locate my passenger, but by the time we had to pull up to spell the car because of the heat we were only 200 miles from home, and the mail finally got through at 9.30 p.m. on Xmas Eve to a reception that could only have been equalled by the Pony Express battling through the Indian war-parties to the beleaguered fort.

We weren't so lucky in our second year in Queensland though, because they are a lot more profligate with their creeks and rivers over here. We knew the mail had got as far as our next-door-neighbour's place but, even discounting the creeks, the bogs were so voracious they'd swallow a tractor whole if it poked its nose out of the shed. We just about needed a snorkel and flippers to get out to read the rain gauge.

Xmas came and went, and by mid-January we'd almost forgotten about the mail. It was a case of forget about "this week, next week" and with luck it will be "sometime".

Pete was ten, and having been denied a place at the Scrabble board where the others whiled away the sodden hours, because he lost his temper when they rejected his purely phonetic spelling, he amused himself putting together a machine which slightly resembled a bicycle, but which did at least allow him more mobility than the rest of us.

When he didn't turn up for lunch one day I queried his absence.

"Oh,” said Mandy vaguely, "I think he was going to try to get over for the mail."

I stopped having hysterics when Sammy threatened to throw a bucket of water over me, but I was still working out the odds on whether he'd get hooked up on a tree trunk or washed right out to sea, when Melissa announced that he was pedalling up the home stretch.

The dripping child announced that he'd swum the creek okay and there was a big mob of mail. He'd picked out his own letters, wrapped them in his shirt and tied it on his head, swum back across the creek and bicycled home.

I had hysterics all over again while he ate a belated lunch and fished cards and postal notes out of his damp envelopes. I don't know whether I was wilder because he might have drowned himself or because it hadn't occurred to the little wretch to at least bring a couple of my letters too.

Letters home

It is that time of year when mothers all over the outback leap with indecent haste upon the incoming mailbag, for yet another batch of incarcerated youth has begun its secondary education at boarding school, and has written its comments home to parents and siblings in either bitterness or resignation, laying the foundation of a correspondence normally of five years' duration, which will run the gamut of every emotion from utter despair to extreme elation.

The era of boarding school letters is one to be treasured by parents; there will never again be experienced such exquisite pleasure, or heart-wrenching sympathy, or vicarious pride, as is occasioned by the receipt of letters from secondary school offspring. (Mainly because by the time they aspire to tertiary studies they have discovered the convenience of the reverse-charge phone call.)

Her child's first term away is the danger period for a mother sitting on the verandah steps sniffing surreptitiously over the pages emanating such misery, explicit or implied. But she must not allow her resolve to be weakened and accede to her kid's request for parole. That misery was only temporary homesickness co-existing with the period of letter-writing, and half an hour after penning it the child was quite likely chatting to its mates or racing around the football field without a care in the world. It's a very rare child who doesn't adapt after the first few weeks.

Letters usually go something like this:

Dear Mum and Dad. . .

"You tought me wrong in long-division. They do it another way here. The boys are all frittened of Stomper, but Curly is all right. He doesn't rock the little kids hard, only rors and pretends to. The food is rotten. . ."

. . . "There is a girl here who says one of the nuns is a werewolf, but I don't think it is true. But she might be. She has sort of pointy teeth. I got 80pc for

maths, but I missed the English test becorse I was sick. Sick bay was lonely so I got better. . ."

. . . "our cooking teacher don't no much, and got very ratty when I told her a better way to make scones. She said show me, so I did, and mine were better and that made her madder still. She said why do I waste my time coming she don't think she can teach me anything. I don't think so either, so can I do carpentry instead of cooking, Mum, then I could mend those chairs Dad won't for you when I come home. I am sad every night but day-time is all right. . ."

. . . "I did not grow like you said I would and the other boys laugh at my shorts, they are to long. I remembered what Dad said, so I picked the biggest one to hit for laughing at me. I hit him on the nose and it bled. He hit me back harder and I bled. The master on duty caned us both for fighting in the dormitory, so we are friends now. His name is Phil. . ."

. . . "I am in the chire, the quire. Well I sing in the chapel on Sunday and we have practice on Thursday nights instead of study-time which is good. Can I have extra fruit from town, everybody has it except me. You have to write to Matron, and she will get it. Smith gave me half of his and I have to pay it back so don't forget. Sometimes I am hungry and I think about rib-bones. We never have rib-bones here, only mince. . ."

. . . "I don't care if Angela and Sybil came to this school, it is no good. They don't teach the things I want to know, only maths and english and pastoral care which is just sticky-beaking. You said not to ask personal questions, but they do. Miss Jones is our pastoral care mistress and I hate her. We had to fill in a form and they arsk things like do your parents live together and are you jeluss of your big brothers and sisters. I am because they don't have to come to this school but I said no. I put that the governess lives with Dad and Mum, and that made me remember you all and the good times at my far-away home and I started to cry though I didn't mean to. She underlined governess and put a red questionmark, I saw it. My friend Peggy says it is none of her bisness. . ."

. . . "There are twins here who change places. They got put in different houses so they couldn't, but they change over beds sometimes, and the masters can't tell. The stitches hurt. I bust one when I stretched. Please send a telegram when the foal comes. I have to know. . ."

. . . "We got pocket money on Saturday morning, and I spent all mine at the tuckshop because I was very hungry. I thort I could get some more today, but alas it was not to be. I have to wait until next Saturday. If I do not larst until then give Trigger to Timmy, and Betty can have my saddle. . ."

. . . "My best friend is Wilma she comes from Nuigini. Her grandfather is the chief of the village, and he is going to get in Parliament. He was a cannibal once, but not now. Wilma wants me to go home with her for the next holidays, but just in case her grandpa is not safe, can I ask her home with me instead?. . ."

. . . Please send $10. Your loving son/daughter. . .

Friends and Neighbours

A night on the town

Norah Twistleton was fed up to the back teeth. Hers was not an overly-suspicious nature, but she felt that it was more than co-incidence that, for the fifth consecutive year, it seemed she and her husband Ted would not be attending the Pastoralists' Dinner-Dance held annually in the nearby town. She was fully aware that Ted had to be laboriously prised off his dung-hill whenever any social occasion loomed, and she conceded that the ratio of bush wives who succeeded in persuading their husbands to accompany the family on holidays was only one to two in favour of those who didn't. But, she reasoned, leaving the station to the tender mercies of the cook or the head-stockman for three or four weeks was a very different prospect to a mere 24 hours absence.

What she resented almost as much as missing the event was the way she always ended up on the defensive in their annual confrontation. There always seemed to be something far more important to be done than gallivanting off to dances. Although Ted never actually used the word "selfish" directly, he skirted around such adjectives as frivolous and sybaritic, and lingered somewhat ominously on "irresponsible attitudes" until Norah frantically begged him not to think that she could be so thoughtless, and apologised profusely for her prior inability to see the situation in its true light. At least, that had been the pattern of the early years of their marriage but too frequent usage finally dimmed the impact and Ted had to resort to various other subterfuges to avoid social appearances. Norah may not have been very bright, but at the end of ten years she had realised that she was the bunny. The stinker just didn't want to go and would descend to any level to get out of it.

Last year when the horse kicked him in the yard he remembered to limp for a full day after the dance date. She ought to have been more suspicious the year he gave in almost at the outset because it was on the very morning of the do that he slipped over in the yards (probably lay down on purpose) and got tramped on by a big snotty-nosed cow. It had to be an act the way he apologised so sincerely between his groans of pain for disappointing her when he knew how much she'd been looking forward to going.

She'd had an accidental win six years ago. Ted woke up with a raging toothache one morning, so Norah grabbed a quick shopping-list and drove him straight to town. After the visit to the dentist he felt so good that when he discovered so many of his mates in town for the dinner-dance he insisted on Norah adding a new dress to her shopping list because it would do her good to have a bit of a fling. He'd enjoyed himself mightily, and on the way home mused that they ought to get out a bit more often. Norah, thankful for small mercies, refrained from braining him with the crank-handle.

But this year Norah was overwhelmed by an obsessive desire to attend that dinner-dance, come hell or high water. She was possibly long past the stage where the thought of dancing really appealed to her: her lip curled contemptuously at the memory of clumsy passes made at her by slightly inebriated males with two left feet. The aim was no longer to dance — it was simply to get there.

The invitation arrived. Norah stuck it on the mantelpiece in a prominent position. When Ted ignored it, she shifted it to his office desk. Still no comment. The card took on a life of its own — on his dressing table, in the bathroom cabinet, on top of the wireless, tacked onto the toilet door. Ted didn't appear to notice. In the Twistleton kitchen Norah made a desperate bid: she fried the card with Ted's steak and plonked the plate down in front of him. He either had to eat it or acknowledge it.

Ted's not the sort of bloke to back away from a challenge. He took the offending card carefully between thumb and forefinger, shook a few drops of gravy from it, pretended to read it, and said "Pity we can't go!"

Next morning he made a positive move. He sent a telegram ordering cattle trucks for the afternoon of and the morning after the dinner-dance. Norah countered in a less forthright manner. Her telegram postponed the trucking one week, and she wrote a fictitious reply in the telegram book, purporting to come from the truckie, saying he was booked up for Ted's date.

Then she set the sewing machine on the dining-room table to make an evening frock, and served meals to the family in the kitchen. Ted's good suit swung on a hanger on the verandah to get the smell of mothballs out of it.

The morning arrived. Ted had decided days before to capitulate, but he'd derived a lot of satisfaction watching Norah simmering while he said nothing. At breakfast he announced, "I have to pick up a new engine, so we may as well stay in for your do." Norah forgave all and rushed for her suitcase.

As they stepped over the threshold of the hall Ted effected a meteoric personality change, exuding conviviality and camaraderie such as to convince all onlookers that he must have been ticking off the days on his calendar.

What unkind fate leads females so unsuspectingly to their doom? Why does the female psyche refuse to acknowledge early-warning signs? Cruel circumstances may ever decree that the dopey female is the designer of her own downfall. Norah began to feel the first prickings of apprehension round about ten o'clock.

Egged on by a couple of schoolmates of long ago Ted had demonstrated his only claim to schoolboy fame by whipping the tablecloth from beneath the glasses and ashtrays. His assertion that the school crockery must have been heavier didn't cut much ice with the caterers.

By eleven "the man who couldn't dance" was corroboree-ing up and down the hall with a dozen other yahoos, bellowing that to do the thing properly they ought to strip off and paint up. The stupid orchestra was encouraging them with a manic beat. The proprietor of the Twistleton acres stopped, panting for breath, beside the table where the mayor's wife sat with antagonistic bosom and steely stare. He caught her gaze, leaned forward beerily and crooned, "Love, you've got beeyootiful eyes — jus' like me best brahman cow!"

At midnight Norah frantically tried to bribe the barman to slip him something guaranteed to cause immediate loss of consciousness, because Ted's bull baritone was announcing that he could ride Curio, Aristocrat, Dargan's grey, and any other yang-yang outlaw wrapped in hide this side of the black stump.

With sinking heart Norah realised that, no yang-yang outlaw being immediately available, it was inevitable that the action would shortly devolve into a bull-fight, that time-honoured finale to many an old-time bush festivity. Many of the ladies were now leaving, casting in Norah's direction glances of either pity or contempt, according to the current state of their friendships.

As Ted and a challenger dropped snorting onto all fours and began pawing the dust on the dance-floor, Norah prayed fervently that the cops would arrive before the furniture began to go. They did.

On the way home Ted said airily, "Only cost me fifty dollars — cheap at the price! We'll have to go out more often, kid — every year from now on, I promise you!"

Norah sniffled agonisingly into her hanky, and Ted, misinterpreting the frightening cauldron of her emotions, took his hand from the steering wheel and laid it affectionately across her shoulder in a gesture of submission, "Okay then, how would every six months suit you!"

Twiss one — Norah nil

Young Twiss is home after all. Don't get the idea that Ted gave in and let him stay. Ted never gives in, even when he's absolutely and utterly wrong; he slides around the situation somehow until it looks as if he's done the right thing, and on odd occasions he's even had the opponents apologising to him and thanking him for putting them on the right track. It's an art Ted has; Norah tries to emulate him sometimes but she always falls flat on her face. However, Twiss may be going to take after Ted.

Young Twiss brought home a mid-semester report that indicated that his heart was not in his studies. It indicated that his hand wasn't either. The modern tendency of teachers is to beat around the bush and write "unco-operative" when they really mean insolent, lazy, and addicted to guerilla-type behaviour; seldom do they even hint that the student has concrete between the ears in that particular area of study. Twiss's headmaster, when signing the report, had forsworn the norm and pencilled-in a note to the form-teacher "Is the boy thick?" and the form-teacher had either forgotten or deliberately omitted to erase it.

Norah was stung to the quick. Maybe Twiss was no Einstein, but he was far from dumb, and she had a swag of Primary School Honour Cards to prove it.

Norah was all for having a good talk to Twiss, and Ted said he would too. Twiss has inherited a certain amount of the paternal cunning, and in preparation for the coming discussion had investigated the old tin trunk and struck pay-dirt — both Ted's and Norah's Secondary School reports, retained in a masochistic belief that posterity demanded the preservation of such incriminating documents.

At the climax of the shouting match the devious youth produced a document which differed from his own report only in the date and Christian name, and minus the pencilled annotation. Cordial relationships were soon re-established and father and son dwelt at length on the inadequacies and intolerances of their respective teachers. The upshot was that Ted decided to drive Twiss back to school himself and have a word with the Headmaster on Twiss's behalf.

It was probably unfortunate that the Headmaster, a recent import from the United Kingdom, had not pursued his colonial experience to the point where he had outgrown the belief that (a) all Australians are scholastically impoverished, and (b) rural Australians are, by virtue of their environment, merely swine before whom it is pointless to cast the pearls of culture and scholarship. Ted gleaned and resented this attitude immediately.

Maybe the Head was patronising to Ted, but he was no coward. Without doubt he won the verbal side of the encounter conclusively, but the honour of the Twistleton's was upheld in the fisticuffs section. The headmaster had learned the Art of Defence at Eton, but Ted had learned his in the stock-camp. Young Twiss, eavesdropping outside the door, broke into a broad grin and loped off to the dormitory to collect his belongings and clean out his locker.

Ted emerged to find him sitting by the car making his farewells to the group of internees who had been his companions of the past three years.

Ted didn't fare half so well in the breaking the news to Norah. She wept hysterically and called her son "an uneducated lout like his father", which was nearly equivalent to the headmaster's considered opinion. The only way they could placate her and avoid bitter recriminations ever after was to promise to enrol the lad at an Agricultural College next year.

In the meantime Twiss is Ted's offsider, and Ted is in the invidious position of having to curb his temper and his comments, so that he can praise his smart son to Norah and uphold the stance he took by pulling Twiss out of school. It is working quite well. Twiss is genuinely enthusiastic and industrious; Ted is learning patience; and Norah is enjoying the growing bond between them. She no longer has to be the buffer between them — in fact it's on the cards that they might even gang-up on her, if the bog incident is any indication.

Last week Ted had a town appointment with the agents, and he left Twiss with instructions to ride the fences on the motor-bike to check on how many trees were down after the recent blow from the cyclone; he reckoned the track would have dried-out enough to get around on the motor-bike.

Twiss forded the creek and skittered around the breakaway until he hit the fence-line. Sure enough the fence was down in the timbered belt, and half-a-dozen sets of tracks led through into the neighbour's place. A big old bloodwood had flattened a full panel of the fence. No way Twiss was going to move that without a chain-saw.

Certainly Ted had told him to take the bike and check, but he hadn't told him not to take the Toyota and fix the damage, and Ted was always stressing initiative. So Twiss rode home, swapped the bike for Toyota and chain-saw, successfully negotiated the creek, and with a spot of low-ratio four-wheel-drive here and there arrived back at the smashed fence.

It took him half-an-hour to operate on the bloodwood, clear the fence-line, and tighten up the panel. Elated with his sense of Mission Completed Satisfactorily, Twiss then embarked impetuously on the fatal step which was to negate his previous success. He had noticed another dead bloodwood close by which the next blow would undoubtedly drop over the fence, and he decided that prevention was better than cure. He was a little power-drunk with the chain-saw in his hand, and his reckoning that the tree would go down parallel to the track if he cut to one side was in direct defiance of the laws of gravity because the tree was already at a 30 degree lean across the track.

It didn't brain Twiss when it came down suddenly because he jumped too fast. It didn't smash the fence either because the Toyota cabin took the full brunt of the fall. A shaken lad retrieved and stopped the chain-saw he'd flung aside and inspected the cabin damage. Nasty. Ted wasn't going to miss that. He levered the tree-trunk off and jumped in, all thought now concentrated on a return home to disguise the damage as best he could. Which impaired his judgement. He backed the Toyota in an arc which dropped it directly and irrevocably into the spewiest piece of ground on the property.

It was lunchtime when he walked in. During the meal he casually announced that he'd like Norah to give him a hand by riding the motor-bike out while he drove the tractor, so she could steer the Toyota when he pulled it out of the bog. Ted never came home in a really good mood after a visit to the agents; Norah knew she had no choice if she wanted to see the father-son relationship maintained at a workable level.

It took an hour to get the Toyota out, and load the bike on the back. Norah, muddy, tired, and aware of the now considerably lower cabin roof over her head and the possibility that the passenger door was never going to open again, mucked up the creek crossing.

Twiss, with a reaction remarkably similar to his father's in times of stress, abused her, manoeuvred the tractor back into the creek bed, and then proceeded to bog it to the eyeballs right alongside the Toyota. It was all they could do to get the bike off successfully, and the return to the homestead with Norah on the pillion was not a pleasant or companionable journey.

Ted got back after sundown and regaled his family with his mediocre but better than usual exchanges with the agents. Norah had dished-up his favourite meal and Twiss was nodding his head appreciatively at Ted's descriptions of his agent-crushing repartee.

"Oh, how were the fences, Twiss?" asked Ted at last. Twiss launched into a description of how he'd removed the bloodwood and fixed the fence, and received Ted's approval for his initiative. Norah carried the dishes out to the kitchen and left Twiss to it.

"Pity you weren't home though, Dad," she heard him say. "Mum did her best but it really needed another man to help when we accidentally bogged the Toyota. Women just aren't strong enough for some jobs, are they!"

When she returned with the coffee Twiss had obviously led up gently to the whereabouts of the tractor, and suggested cleverly that it would be the work of a moment to rescue it in the morning now that Big Strong Man was home to replace Poor Little Weak Woman who'd bogged the Toyota that caused the bogging of the tractor. Norah's sense of Justice and her Mother Instinct warred momentarily, but Mother Instinct won. After all, Twiss still had to explain away the bashed-in cabin, though she had little doubt that, while working together in male camaraderie in the morning, he would find some plausible and blame-free explanation.

So she handed the big strong males their coffee, accepting stoically that what a female loses on the roundabouts of Justice she usually makes up on the swings of Peaceful Coexistence.

Chez Twistleton

Eunice Chetwynd is giving us all a pain in the neck. If Godfrey doesn't keep a tighter rein on her, his bank manager is going to have the last laugh after all. Nobody could blame her for wanting a new homestead, but a conservatory, I ask you! A side verandah fenced in with green glass and all rigged up with a sprinkler system, stuffed full of potted palms, urns and jars of spotted leaves and exotic blooms, and a rather ornate metal table and chairs where Eunice now entertains her visitors for smoko.

When they visited last weekend Ted Twistleton was rather impressed by the new barbecue on the lawn, but Norah drew comfort from his comment on the way home that he hadn't enjoyed drinking his tea with a bunch of triffids breathing down his neck. With all the scrub Godfrey had on the place outside the back door he couldn't see why they wanted to invite its toney relations to take over the inside.

Norah, who had side-stepped Eunice's magnanimous offer to strike her some cuttings once she had established the right environment for the delicate plants, was considering whether there was any point in purchasing a pack of the plant food, which Eunice had recommended, for the sickly pot of jade which clung to life precariously on top of the Twistleton fridge. Her sister-in-law had given it to her months before, thick-leaved and flourishing, assuring her of its hardiness and warning her that it would probably burgeon to such an extent that she would need to divide it and start a colony. The sad thing wilted despondently on the fridge and periodically cast down showers of fat yellowing leaves, so that Norah was for ever reaching for the dustpan.

In a burst of healthy reaction Norah considered instead how she might lay hands on a pot of marijuana and introduce it surreptitiously into the Chetwynd's floral opulence, but her daydreams were interrupted when she had to get out and open the gate, collect the mail from the mail-box, and return to the more pressing details of her mundane existence, like getting tea for the family in a kitchen that lagged behind Eunice's stunningly modern cul-de-sac by three decades or so.

Reading the papers after tea brought no balm to the stirry Twistleton soul. In Australia's caste system they undoubtedly belonged to the Untouchables, members of the down-trodden agricultural community, victimised on every side. "Grow food," growled Ted, "and every man and his dog considers you fair game. You feed the sods, and they go all-out to stop you! Can't clear this bit of land — can't fish here — can't brand your stock in case it hurts `em — can't buy a bit of land because old King Didgerydoo lit his campfire on it in 1820 — can't do this, can't do that! And now it's Land Rights for Yellow Dogs — I ask you!"

As the last light was distinguished and the Twistletons pulled up the covers a chorus of dingo wails arose from all points of the perimeter of the homestead.

"We're besieged," shivered Norah, "and their reinforcements are coming up with the Conservation mob. Ted's right — we are Untouchables!"

Now if you are going to wake up sour on any particular morning of the week, it's more likely to be a Monday. Norah got up to face a larger than usual weekly wash in an elderly wringer-type machine, not even distantly related to Eunice Chetwynd's wash-rinse-dry-and probably fold-up and put-away-in-the-wardrobe impressive model.

Having Young Twiss home doubled the load of dirty working clothes and trebled the mending and. . . . Resolutely she had another cup of coffee and pulled herself together.

She was just pegging Twiss' second pair of overalls in the last space left on the bed-linen line when the wire strung between two gum trees snapped. So did Norah's resolve.

Ted and Twiss drove home for lunch and into the vortex of a force ten domestic disagreement.

"You think nothing of ordering a hundred rolls of barbed wire," she accused Ted, "but a hundred yards of no. 8 is good enough for me to hang out your dirty laundry! I've been wanting a laundry hoist for so long it's not funny, but oh no, the calves need a new branding cradle, Twiss has to have a new saddle, the workshop gets a new grinder. If your old stud bull gets a sore pizzle, you can't call the vet in quick enough, but if I fell down the back steps and broke a leg I wouldn't be surprised if you sent Twiss inside for the .22 and shot me!"

Norah didn't sound off very often but when she did, she did it properly, and she was obviously laying on canvas for a fine sprint downwind.

"You talk about Untouchables in the bush!" she screeched. "I'm the Untouchablest of the lot!"

"Would there be such a word as untouchablest?" mused Young Twiss, in a laudable endeavour to improve his understanding of the English language — an honest enquiry, certainly, but not timed diplomatically.

"You little creep!" snarled Norah, turning on him, "you and your father can wash your own untouchable laundry after this, and peg it up on your own rotten barbed-wire too, because I won't be doing it!"

At this stage Ted tried his normally successful placatory approach, and sidled up to the virago at the sink with hands outstretched and a soppy smile on his face. He slid his arms around her waist, and started to say "Fair go, darling, we wouldn't —" but she cow-kicked him viciously on the shin and then whirled round and sloshed him across the face with the dish-cloth, burst into tears, and rushed into the bedroom, slamming the door so violently that the old-fashioned door-knob fell off with a clatter. (Eunice had sliding doors on her master-bedroom.)

While the family were still gawping at the rolling door-knob the door burst open again, and Norah rushed out, seized the ailing jade from the fridge, wrenched open the back door, and hurled the pathetic plant at the laundry door, where it burst asunder in a salvo of leaves, dirt, and shards of green pot. Then she walked firmly to the bedroom, entered, and kicked the door shut.

Something more than displays of affection or wordy flattery on Ted's part was needed to heal this breach: he wasn't going to get out of it under anything less than a new clothes-hoist. So on Tuesday he drove to town and bought it, and Twiss threw in for a large box of chocolates dolled up with a shiny blue ribbon.

Ted and Twiss erected the silver sweetheart on Wednesday morning, and a somewhat mollified Norah slipped a pavlova into the oven as a peace-offering for Young Twiss, who may yet be diverted from becoming as overtly chauvinistically-male as his pa.

When the job was finished, and Ted grinningly produced a new laundry trolley and basket from the boot of the car, she capitulated entirely, and made his favourite wine trifle for dessert. Chateau Twistleton was back to normal.

It looked like rain on Friday, and the atmosphere was heavy and still, almost oppressive. Ted said he wouldn't be surprised if there wasn't a hail-storm in the offing. Norah hoped it would rain because, apart from anything else, the garden could do with a freshen-up.

During Friday night they didn't get more than twenty points of rain, but they did get one of the fiercest twisters they'd had in years.

The twister uprooted gum trees for half a mile along the horse-paddock fence and cut right across the Twistleton backyard. Miraculously it left the T.V. aerial untouched, but it bent Norah's new clothes-hoist parallel to the ground and twisted one cross-arm up into the air like an injured umbrella frame.

On Sunday morning Twiss got some no. 8 wire and put up a temporary clothes-line for his mother between two still-standing gum trees. When Eunice Chetwynd rang up at smoko-time to invite Norah to pop over for the afternoon, she had every reason to complain later to Godfrey that Norah Twistleton's manner of refusal had been positively curt.

The *House* of the Thousand Cleanskins

My kingdom

While Joe and I are of similar mind on most subjects, such as politics, religion, and raising children, we do have this slight difference of opinion on priorities since taking up the brigalow block.

Joe says you must get your priorities right, and we composed our first list sitting in the cabin of a bogged vehicle ten miles short of our destination, in the middle of what later became know as Toyota Wallow, during the three inch downpour which heralded our introduction to the first of many cyclones.

for a house

The list read: camp, motor bike, tractor, fencing, yards, breeders, stud bulls.

Subsequent lists over the ensuing twelve months always had 'house' listed as no. 14. In the light of my present situation, Lord knows where I'd be now if it had been no. 13.

During my callow youth my peer group often referred to me as naive. I preferred to think that I was endowed, rather, with a trusting nature.

However, it is only a fortnight since Mandy used the same term when discussing my expectations regarding the possible erection of THE HOUSE.

But I remain optimistic. It is now no. 6 on the priorities list.

For the first year I didn't mind the absence of a conventional dwelling in the least. Our eight-bay bough shed was air-conditioned, photogenic, and I had for many years nurtured the belief that if I had been born a century earlier the demands of a pioneering existence would not have found me wanting, and here was a chance to test myself.

We already owned a set of flat-sided billycans and a medium-sized camp-oven, and Joe gave me a large camp-oven and a long-handled shovel for Christmas.

Sammy fashioned a neat set of hooks from No. 8 wire to go with them. The added bonus to campfire cooking was that I never had a failure with my bread, which had never happened before, and, I regret to report, has not happened since.

Pete, aged nine, didn't altogether approve of my forethought in bringing along an old school desk and a tin trunk of correspondence lessons and text books, but became fairly tractable when it was explained to him that the option was boarding school.

After twelve months in the bough-shed, the erection of a machinery shed with temporary living quarters was a great step forward, and Joe insists that I wore a pad a foot deep round the second-hand wood stove strategically placed outside the back door, as I walked around it and patted it on the chimney pipe.

Well, maybe I did, but after six years I'm not as thrilled about it all as I was then, and that's an understatement.

The recession kept me quiet for four years, but I've been working myself up over the past eighteen months, as new dams, new fences, new bulls, new stockhorses, and old creditors keep my dream home locked about midway down the list of priorities.

Some years ago the Women's Weekly published a quiz relating to whether your home was executive or humpy status. Being categorised hinged, as far as I can remember, on the number of flash chandeliers and the measurements of bookshelves (complete with books, please) which your home boasted.

Joe uses this system whenever I get that hard-done-by look in my eyes. It is useless for me to compare three round tin light-shades and a Dolphin torch to the required eight chandeliers for an upper-crust establishment, when he can counter with one hundred and fourteen feet of filled bookshelves plus four large tin trunks of overflow, compared to the six feet of books mandatory for big-shots.

The woman's touch to any home must, I think, include curtains at the windows, and a garden with flowers in it as well as vegetables. When we build the house Joe is going to put a fence around it to protect the garden from the stock.

I haven't got much of a garden yet because it has to be watered by buckets from the shed tank, and after Joe's best stud bull ate three large banana trees and five pawpaws down to stumps I felt somewhat resentful. When it snapped off the about-to-bear mango tree I got stinking mad.

Throwing rocks at it was never going to deter that creature. It paid its fateful visit when Joe was to be absent from home for a fortnight.

I'll swear I only meant to frighten it. But the sight of it leering in the open end of the shed with half a sweetcorn plant drooping wanly from its chomping mouth sent me berserk. I grabbed the 303, steadied it on the kitchen table, aimed three inches above its head, and pulled the trigger.

I fell over backwards, and the bull fell over forwards, right into the shed and onto the new motor-bike.

I didn't have a vehicle to haul the carcase away. The next day I had to take the old motor-bike and some camping gear and shift down to the bore.

When Joe got home ten days later I thought maybe he'd move the house up the priorities list, like right now, number one, because it was by then the ripest machinery-shed and temporary living quarters in the whole of Queensland.

But he didn't. He said he'd had such a good break that he could tackle anything, and if the little woman liked to put on a feed at the camp with the goodies he'd brought back, he'd nip up and make the old place habitable again in no time, and not to worry, that bull was beginning to get past it, and he'd seen the agent about some new bulls while he was away.

It was after the stove died that I began to get obsessive about the house. The stove had bravely weathered cyclonic rains, ordinary wets, and a variety of competent and incompetent cooks.

When the right-hand end fell off, and two weeks later the oven door, it was purely because of old age.

Mandy, capable creator of scones, roasts, baked tarts, and delicious cakes, registered distress, and I grew hopeful when the boss said it wasn't worth getting a new second-hand stove when we'd need a brand-new gas stove inside the house, and instructed Mandy in the art of pot-roasting for the time being.

A month later the first heavy shower of last wet finished the stove entirely.

A yell from Pete, who was standing at the doorway, brought us all rushing to witness the demise. Stove went over backwards, almost in slow motion, spewing coals from the firebox and our bathwater from the two-gallon boiler on top. We gazed in shock at the death-throes.

Everything except the copper side-fountain and the chimney pipe disintegrated before our eyes, and suddenly stove was no more than a grey-black sodden mound of metal, ash, and soot.

Coupled with my sadness at such a pathetic end to a faithful servant was a guilty rush of exultation at the thought that now we'd have to get the house to put the new stove in.

I am always under-estimating Joe. Within twenty-four hours he had installed on the same spot a slow-combustion stove and hot-water tank which someone threw out years ago when the power lines went through.

"This should last for years," he said, as he tightened up the hot-water tap. And I think the wretched thing probably will!

House on the horizon

I was sulking on the bed when I heard the girls returning from the yards where they'd been helping their father brand the latest mob of cleanskins. "What's the matter with Mum?" I heard Mandy say. "She's getting around like a frog with a broken leg." "Just like an old catfish stranded on the bank of the lagoon, the way she's snapping at everyone," agreed Melissa.

More like a cut snake than a catfish the way I came up off that bed.

"A bit more filial respect round here would go a long way!" I snarled, kicking the door shut in their faces, so that Mandy leapt back startled onto her sister's foot, causing Melissa to jump around and screech.

"If you let us in," yelled Mandy, "we'll make you a cuppa and let you earbash us!"

"We've been working since sun-up — we need our smoko. Come on, Mum, fair go!" begged Melissa.

I relented, and made smoko. After all, it wasn't their fault that their father kept doing sums aloud and figuring on the backs of old envelopes, estimating how much clearing he could do when this mob was sold, or whether to put in another dam, or a new set of yards with laneways.

"Mum," said Mandy, sipping her tea and patting my hand, "you come in every time. Haven't you woken up to Dad yet? He couldn't pull that teasing stunt on me since I was six years old!"

Melissa chimed in. "You can't teach an old dog new tricks, Mandy. Oops — sorry, Mum."

Joe carried on the theme a few minutes later when he strolled in.

"Gotta throw you a bone now and then, Mum," he said, tossing a second-hand envelope into my lap. It was the Priorities List, the new one. It began on the back with no. 2 — Yards, no. 3 — Laneway, and so on. Mystified, I turned it over, and in big letters scrawled beside our name on the front was

's HOUSE — no. 1.

You've seen an excited dog racing round and round in circles, yapping and leaping, haven't you? Well, that was me, hugging the brute, and laughing and dancing round in circles.

He'd already burnt out some stumps on the house-site, and I'd registered the smoke, but in my sour pessimism I'd presumed that he was burning off rubbish, or making smokes for the horses, or practicing smoke signals.

Wives who have clawed their way up the cliff face of camp, shed, or caravan-living are well aware of the elation one experiences at the announcement of the new homestead on the horizon.

Be it ever so humble, there's no place like home, but that's only if you can't get a flash one. Replacement of humble dwellings by new homesteads may be effected in a variety of ways, including fires, floods, cyclones, white ants, or chronic nagging. Being patient takes a little longer.

This is perhaps the place to discuss humble outback homes for those wives who enjoy the nostalgic flashback, while feeling confidently secure in the knowledge that they are unlikely to have to repeat the experience.

Drovers' wives had a humble camp — a new one nearly every night. They kept their worldly possessions in boxes on the back of the truck or dray. I knew one who carried a carefully-packed Royal Doulton dinner service, a wedding present from her parents in London, on the tray of the truck just aft of the saddles and swags.

Early Settlers' wives began in a tent, followed by a bough shed, and then a hut. Huts are still around, but today they have tin roofs in common with homesteads. The walls may be corrugated iron or antbed. Thick ant-bed is preferable, because it is cooler in summer, and warmer in winter. Ant-bed is also used for floors by some, while others claim that a mixture of ashes and cow-dung is superior.

The modern new settler has a caravan, then a small shed, followed by a large shed.

The main disadvantage common to all these humble dwellings is that it is impossible to draw a clear distinction between domestic and working lives. In the droving camp one might conceivably be stepped on by a bullock while asleep, or wake to find the night-horse has stolen the breakfast damper. The bed in the hut has the tool-box stored beneath it, and the station books or the saddling thread and wax must be pushed to the far end of the table in order to set out a meal. The horse liniment brushes shoulders with the tomato sauce in the caravan cupboard, and the carburettor is dissected on the van table. The office work is always done there, and it is not uncommon to find fencing pliers, spanners, or ear-mark pliers lurking on the seats, especially when visitors call. In the large shed one may sleep cheek by jowl with a yellow bulldozer, misplace the spare bed under a pile of saddles, shift bags of cement to reach the washing machine, discover a rifle or a branding iron in the wardrobe, and dingo scalps under the washtub.

As Joe and I pored together over the plans for The House of the Thousand Cleanskins, I noted his beatific smile and commented happily, "You're just as pleased as I am, aren't you?"

"Sure am," he grinned. "It'll be great to get all this household stuff out of my shed, so I can get a clear go and set up a decent workshop without tripping over armchairs and potplants all the time."

The priorities battle

Joe escaped and got into town last week with a cheque book, and spent two K of cleanskins in one hit. Armed with a list of requirements to provide water and plumbing for The House of the Thousand Cleanskins he began soberly enough, ordering overhead tank, rainwater tanks and various piping and whatever to provide hot and cold at the requisite outlets in kitchen, laundry and bathroom.

My contribution to his list was merely the colour and shape of the taps; all those pipes and bends and so on are quite beyond my comprehension. Obviously he had to go to town to do the purchasing because, as far as I am concerned, the water begins at the tap and ends at the plug-hole. There is no way I could have discussed plumbing with the salesman at the establishment which handles such dull merchandise.

It wasn't dull to Joe though. Neither is he as single-minded as I am. He sees the broad perspective, and where I now see only "The House", his vision encompasses the whole station. It also encompasses the whole stock of that establishment: stock-tanks, troughing, engines, pumps, windmills, nuts, bolts, cement — and, flushed with a heady rush of power to the hip-pocket, he rearranged the priorities I hadn't yet got around to telling him about.

In my naive imagining, one cleanskin bull equalled loungeroom curtains; two or three mickies, say, a nice colonial suite; and throw in another couple for a flash carpet. Silly girl! Cleanskin bulls equal cement tanks; they are legal tender for pumps and troughs; they are equivalent of diesel engines.

As long as I can forestall another imminent trip to town, maybe I can salvage one K of cleanskins and divert the proceeds to furniture. If I get to sort the mail first, I can mislay the farm machinery catalogues or file them under L for Later. All's fair in the battle of priorities, as every farm wife knows, and who's worried about being fair, anyway?

Once you've quelled any slight prickings of conscience and firmly excised the logical reasons why the station needs should come first, there are a number of devious moves you can make to get your own wilful way.

Lying to machinery salesmen who call when your husband is out on the run is a good start. Ply them with cups of tea and work the conversation round to overdrafts, and babble on about creditors dunning at your door.

"Oh, thank goodness," you can say. "I thought you were the man from (preferably their business rivals) come about the payments on the (tractor, harvester, etc.)." As soon as you see their eyes start to slide sideways, and they murmur about having to make a move, you know their enthusiasm for a prospective sale is waning. But don't get over-confident and over-do it, because they might meet your husband on the road out, and you want to be able to cover your tracks if you're caught out.

Another ploy is learning to handle neighbours who have been acting like the last of the big spenders in station improvements, and drop in on Sunday morning to skite about their latest acquisitions and invite your husband to call over and see for himself these time-, labour- and money-saving devices which make the job of the man on the land a comparative piece of cake. Finesse needed here. The actual neighbouring windmill in action compared to your rickety old pump-jack hiccoughing over the bore is a far greater adversary than mere, pretty, coloured pictures on a salesman's brochure.

This situation requires the subtle inference in a subsequent conversation with your husband that the neighbour's mediocre managerial ability is such that he could not effectively do his job without all this new equipment, whereas there are others who can manage a far better result with a minimum of gear.

Sulking when a tonne of barbed wire replaces the garden furniture you'd planned is definitely out; so is playing the martyr. You win some and you lose some. Wipe the scorecard clean and conserve energy for the next round.

And for me, there is always the compensation of the unexpected, the tantalising puzzle: what will he bring home this time?

I know what he plans to purchase because I help him make the lists. If it's urgent station gear, I know that will certainly appear, but it's the "maybe we ought to think about it. . ." suggestions that don't always come to fruition.

Like the time he went to an auction to buy a lawnmower and came home with 48 school desks. And the intended purchase of a kids' pony which resulted in 103 stockhorses milling around the backdoor. And the huge radiogram with strong communist ties — Radio Peking on six channels — that was supposed to be an electric iron.

And with them all comes Joe's unbeatable brand of logic. The desks were unloaded on the lawn because there was nowhere else to put them. With the desks there we couldn't mow it, could we, so we didn't need a mower, did we?

Movement at the station

Well, it's that time of year again, and all the property chores to be done; plugging up the gun barrels so that hornets can't build nests inside them; laying in supplies of citronella ahead of the vicious warcries of the Scotch Greys and their attendant hordes of Tartar sandflies; making votive offerings to the Gods of Nature to allow the mail to get through with the postal votes and out again with the completed ballot papers.

There are two good omens that there will be a Wet Season this year, and the first is an election and referendum. Elections have nothing to do with three-year terms. Government of whatever shade are wary of stirry Northern pastoral representations, so they call elections when the possibility of pastoralists being able to get to polling booths is at its lowest. Drought time, no election: wet season and floods, election whether it's due or not. I haven't worked out yet how they know the weather ahead of time, but my statistical research of past election dates and weather dates shows beyond reasonable doubt that it has to be more than happy co-incidence.

For my second omen I fall back on Aboriginal lore. Last Friday I saw a plain-turkey with the biggest show of mating plumage that I've ever seen — he was a veritable giant of strutting male supremacy, an arrogant king calling imperiously to his meek and dutiful little hens. The Aborigines say that a male turkey on a sex binge is a sure sign of big rains soon, and the bigger the plumage the bigger the rains. The fact that I found a scattered pile of feathers on Saturday which indicated that a dingo had sent him to his Maker with his sexual appetites unappeased was not, I believe, a sign that the prospects of rain may be reversed, but rather a placatory gesture to the anti-male sex-discriminators who are now so loud in the land.

So with the supply of water pretty well assured for the plant and animal life, we turn next to the human requirements — the water supply for the House of the Thousand Cleanskins. On Saturday the transport arrived, and half the loading was for the house. That came off the truck first, and while I couldn't rouse the ultimate in enthusiasm for the rolls of polythene piping, lengths of steel, bags of bolts, and crated tank parts that would eventually be a squatter's tank on a tower, I could certainly get enthused over the two ready-made rain-water tanks for each corner of the back verandah. When they were lifted off and placed on their shining sides on the flat I rushed over and stroked them lovingly. They were real; the rest still had to be put together.

Then we had to unload the animals' share at a dam a few miles away. They got more piping, some troughing, a pump, and one of those circular cement troughs which came off last. While the driver operated the crane Joe climbed inside the trough to adjust the chains. The driver touched the lever, and I saw the momentary indecision on Joe's face but it was too late for him to leap out with anything other than an undignified scramble. So he gave a nonchalant wave of the hand as he rode it to the ground, assuming at the same time an expression that was meant to make me believe he'd intended to do just that all the time.

There looked to be a fair storm brewing, so we farewelled the loading driver and made tracks for home. If we hadn't stopped on the way to let down a panel of fence and hunt back a young bull who'd got into the wrong paddock, we might have beaten the wind which was a prelude to the coming storm. As the first gusts hit us, Joe let out a yelp — "The rain-water tanks!" and jumped into the vehicle so fast that it was just luck that I had time to hurl myself in too.

The vehicle and the wind made about equal time up the ridge, but the wind put on enough of a spurt ahead of us to get the tanks moving just before we screeched to a halt. One tank caroomed into the other and sent it bowling across the flat. Joe raced to get in the lead, throwing his hat down in front of it to turn it. It ignored both his yells and his hat, and flattened the latter.

(That didn't really matter, because Joe's hats have a chequered career, and frequently have to be shoved back into his particular, easily-recognised style.)

Meantime I ran in circles round the other tank, keening and cursing alternately. The two dogs also ran round in circles, barking delightedly at the new game. Those tanks are eight feet across the base, and up-ended on its side one of them can be a pretty formidable assailant if you're galloping in front of it yelling whoa. A minute before I hadn't been in front; I'd been behind it with my arms out full-stretch, though I still hadn't worked out what to do when I caught it. Then the wind did a sudden switch at the same moment as the tank collided with a tree, from which it rebounded with such alacrity that if I hadn't reversed as smartly as I did it would've caught me. Straight ahead was the verandah, and the tank lumbered after me like a juggernaut. I jumped up with a dog on either side of me, and the behemoth clanked against the verandah and came to a standstill. I grabbed a couple of planks to anchor it, and then turned panting to check on its mate.

Across the flat the second outlaw tank had met its match. (Well, the wind had dropped, if you like it better that way.) It was trundling meekly home, cowed and beaten, while the Man from Cattle Camp never slackened in his stride.

So we yarded them, meek as milkers now, flat on their bases the way all good tanks should go, and as the first raindrops spattered down, we retired to put the billy on for a well-earned smoko.

You Win Some,
You Lose Some.

One straight-jacket coming up!

It's an ill-wind that blows nobody good. The Government decision to do away with the Diesel Fuel Certificates which allowed for a cheaper price for on-farm diesel has an important side benefit. We have filled out the last of those rotten Customs forms. I don't know yet whether the Rebate form will be as difficult, because, try as I might, I can't track down such a thing. I distinctly heard the announcement on the radio that we would probably have the rebate organised before the fuel bill fell due at the end of the month, but, although we paid our bill four months ago, there's no sign yet of any rebate application form. I, for one, have decided it is probably worth paying the extra price to avoid filling in the form. (Good thinking on the Treasurer's part. I bet I'm not the only one.)

However, we had to submit the Customs form from January to August, 1982, to show how much diesel we'd bought at the exempt price and how much we'd bought at the full price, and how much we'd used on the station and how much for private use. Actually, we hadn't bought any. We'd got a twelve-months supply the previous November, paid an estimated percentage at the full price and the rest at the exempt price, and pumped the whole lot into the diesel tank.

The uninitiated might think that a one-page questionnaire, when you haven't bought any fuel, should be relatively easy to answer. Ha! For a start, the form asks the questions in miles and gallons, the speedo on the vehicle reads in kilometres, and the Oil Company sells in litres.

There are frustrated form-collectors all over Australia who can back-up my statement that Joe was a form-procrastinator even in the good old days when we only had a couple of dozen per annum. He would avoid the odious chore to

within an inch of the $100 fine or six months in jail; he would make the senders run through the whole gamut of the polite "perhaps you have forgotten" letters, to the "wish to draw your attention" statements, right up to the "it is an offence" outright-nasty ones.

Now that he has mellowed with time he only makes a token gesture of defiance now and then; he was always prepared to take on a Government Department in the old days, but it's no longer a fair fight with all those computers as well as the clerks.

He began the Customs form in a mood of muted resignation. We all helped him.

"How many miles to the gallon does the Toyota do?"

"Say 24."

"What's that in kilometres and litres?"

"Well, it doesn't matter, does it? The form is in miles."

"Yes, but I've got to fill in the speedo reading, and the speedo's in kilometres."

The maths wizard, Pete, converted in his head, and Mandy checked it with the calculator.

"But that's not the speedo reading! I'm suppose to put the true speedo reading!"

"For last August? — How are you going to do that?"

"Well, dear, you only went to town twice in the Toyota during that time.

At 24 miles to the gallon. . ."

"Kilometres to the litre—"

"It's obvious we've paid full price for six times that distance, so why don't you say that somewhere, and that should satisfy them!"

"Well, it won't. I've got to work it out."

He worked it out. I can't say whether it was right or not. Pete had gone out to feed his dog, and Mandy was reading. She looked up suddenly.

"Don't forget," she said, "that it's not 120 miles to town at the full price."

"What do y'mean! Of course it is!"

"No, it's eight miles to the front gate. That's a private road. Private roads are exempt price."

"Don't mix me up. I was on private business, wasn't I!"

"Yes, but you were on private business on a private and a public road, and you only have to pay the public price when you're on private business on the public bit of road, because on the private bit you could have been checking the fence as well as being on private business, so you needn't pay the public price, see!"

"Say that again!"

"No! Don't let her say it again! Go and read your book, Mandy."

Joe was starting to breathe heavily. I poured him a cup of tea, and enquired sweetly, "Well, how many gallons does that come to, dear?"

Mandy was a bit piqued. "Bet he doesn't know" she muttered sotto voce.

"Even if he does, it's not right, because there's eight miles. . ."

"Mandy!"

Pete came in, looked over Joe's shoulder, shook his head, and said, "Look, Dad, why don't you say you went to town in Mum's bus. That's petrol. How do they know what you went to town in, or even if you went at all?"

"I've got to use up some of the stuff I bought, don't I!"

"I've got to put here how much I've still got on hand for both exempt price and full price. And what I've used has to tally with how much of each I had on Jan 1st 82, and how much of each I had on hand in August 82."

"How much did you have of each, dear?"

"How the hell would I know? It's all mixed up together in the one tank, isn't it!"

"Do you want me to get a dipstick, Dad, and measure what we've got left" offered Pete. "I can do the volume sum for you, and get it in gallons."

"For last August," sneered Mandy, looking up from the station diary which she was now perusing. "How are you going to add on what we've used between August and now?"

Pete gave her a dirty look. Joe went on making calculations on the back of an envelope. Mandy flicked over the pages, and then gave a yelp of triumph.

"I thought so," she said, "that second trip you did, it wasn't 120 miles. Remember, it was wet, and it says here you had to take the wet-weather road, so that's 145 miles, okay? That means you did 33 miles on a private road, at the exempt price. Of course, being in four-wheel-drive you would have used more than 24 miles to the gallon. And you got bogged. That'd use up more, wouldn't it? There, I've saved you some of the dear stuff, haven't I?"

"Mandy, I don't want to save it. I just want to write down what happened to it!"

"What you ought to do, Dad," volunteered Pete, "is keep the two lots separate, and only use the full-price stuff when you go to town."

"Yeah, like I drain the tank of the exempt stuff, fill up with the other, and write down the mileage before I leave, and then when I get home again I drain out the full-price fuel, put it back in the drum, write down the mileage. . ."

"At the gate," said Mandy primly, "you'd have to do all that at the gate too! It's eight miles. . ."

"Pete," I said, "there'd be no point in doing that anyway now. We have to pay full price for the lot since last August."

"Yes, but you'll still have to work it out for the rebate forms!"

"Not," said Joe, as he picked up his form and stood up, "if I trade-in the diesel vehicle for a petrol one. Then it will all be rebate!"

He walked out, went over to the shed, and locked himself in — or us out, I'm not sure which.

Anyway, I posted the completed form last mail. I'm going to leave it a couple of weeks before I give him the census forms that were in the incoming mail.

Holiday traumas

At this point in time (got a ring to it, hasn't it? All the best politicians use it frequently!) or, as the bushies say — Right now — not many self-employed rural dwellers have either the wherewithal or the time to indulge themselves in that employee-class luxury, the annual holiday. It is no use bemoaning the fact that you can't afford a spell, but you are quite entitled to remonstrate gently with the mealy-mouthed twit who suggests that a change is as good as a holiday, when your change has been a meteoric one from the horse-yards where you were breaking-in to the fractures ward of the local hospital.

There are two angles from which to consider holidays when you obviously aren't going to get one in the foreseeable future.

The optimistic way is where you buy a casket ticket and plan what you'll do when you win. You have to go for the half-million casket, because either your conscience or your partner is going to swallow nine-tenths of it paying off the debt, putting in dams, buying tractors, refurnishing the house, up-grading the herd, and so on.

You have to start with the amount you want for the holiday, deduct that, and then let the conscience and/or spouse play with the remainder. If you think you'll have the remainder for the holiday you're done before you're off the ground. Husbands mad with Improvements Mania can dispose of a measly Treasure Chest win in the first fifteen minutes before you've even had time to produce the newspaper with the ads for the cut-price tourist trips in the off-season.

Another tip. Don't forget the holiday extras, like paying the wages of the caretaker-manager, and the cost of a holiday wardrobe. If you haven't had a holiday for a few years you are going to find that there is only one place where you can save money with the current "appropriate dress for the occasion"; that's on the beach. You can now go starkers if you like, and you won't be run in, so that's a hundred percent saving on bathing costumes. Bet you're not game, though! The tanned parts you've already got would immediately pin-point where you came from, and a beachful of brindled bushies or piebald pastoralists would undoubtedly draw more than a passing glance.

Having ear-marked a substantial sum, do the thing on a grand scale. Go overseas — New Zealand, Fiji, Noumea. After all, it's not going to cost you anything — you're only day-dreaming. This is reasoned advice. If you go to an Australian capital, you'll find so many changes you'll feel like a foreigner, and probably make a fool of yourself. You may as well go somewhere where you are a foreigner, and they make allowances for it.

If you've already exhausted that scheme, you can try the other approach — the pessimistic one. You go right back over all the holidays you've ever had, and you dredge up all the things that went wrong. It's amazing how many lousy things have happened on holidays, especially if you write them down on a list. You can even have separate headings to help you remember, such as Weather, Finance (that's a goody!), In-laws, Illnesses, Mucked-up Itineraries, Strikes, and Sundries. All these can be broken down into sub-headings: Weather: (a) on the way, (b) there, (c) back home (e.g. a cyclone while you're away, but the phone's out, so you can't contact them to find out if the roof is still on the homestead, but it probably isn't from the weather reports). Finance: (a) casinos/race-tracks, (b) boutiques/furniture stores, (c) delusions of grandeur in the Farm Machinery showrooms, (d) unexpected motor vehicle repairs, (e) entertainment, licit and illicit, (f) bribing offspring. In-laws: (a) doddering aunties, (b) socialist brothers-in-law, (c) nymphomaniac cousins, (d) con-men who want to sell you shares, (e) black sheep who would be able to reform if only you'd find a job for them on that lovely big station; of course, if they'd only had the chance that you'd had. . .

Under Sundries you can list losing the children in the chain store, Johnny bitten by the zebra at the zoo, Mum encouraging the attentions of that suave ex-boy-friend until you were forced to thump him under the ear at the barbecue, Mum staying at her girl-friend's place until you apologised, and you getting arrested when you honestly thought it was the Avis car you'd just rented, and when you came out of the pub and the keys were in it, you naturally just got in and drove away. And so on.

When you have noted everything nasty that has ever happened to you, you then add the awful things that holidaying friends and neighbours have suffered, and finish off with everything that went wrong at home while you were away.

In some cases, what went wrong at home is enough in itself to put you off the whole idea. Like when the caretaker went into town and got on the grog, and the bore broke down and perished a mob of cattle. Or when the bushfire burnt the homestead you'd just bought the new furniture for.

With everyone in the family pulling their weight, you can soon reach a final assessment that the last thing you need in these days of trial and tribulation is another dose of holiday trauma. Everyone will agree that holidays are vastly over-rated, and the opinion will hold until the family gets a visit from city friends on long-service leave, touring Australia and having a whale of a time. . .

"What's that, dear?"

"You actually won the lucky draw of the month at the Tractor Sales and Repairs place?"

"A trip for two to Brisbane, or a thousand dollars cash!"

"You chose the cash, and got them to deduct it from the cost of the repairs!"

"YOU WHAT!!!"

Social survey in the scrub

I note with interest that the burgeoning Survey Industry has now burst out of the city and suburbs, and is panting hot on the trail of yet another "unique" group, i.e. remote grazing families, whose quality of life is to be examined in a survey to be launched after a trial survey to see if there is anything worth surveying. The actual mechanics of making a survey is a fairly simple affair. All they have to do is sit down and work out a questionnaire, post same to every tenth name in the relevant part of the phone book, and collate the results when about 10% of the questionnaires are returned. It's the mugs on the other end who have to do all the hard work.

But I begin to see a snag with the current survey on the quality of life of remote grazing families. Apart from filling in the questionnaire, the victim has to keep a diary for a set period on "the amount of travel away from the station, visitors, and the daily work program". For a start, you know who is going to say "Okay, we'll be in it" and you know who is going to do the hackwork of filling in the forms and keeping the diary, and it isn't going to be him.

Questionnaires are ticklish things at the best of times: the answers depend on the mood you're in at the time, and/or what political, economic, or emotional ulterior motive you might have. Let's take a random sample from the typical day of a station wife. ("I'm too busy — gotta muster Big Bluebush this week — you'll write up that stuff, won't you, love!")

Questionnaire (extract)

Q. Do you employ a governess?

A. No. She shot through with the head-stockman last week.

Q. Do your secondary school children attend boarding school?

A. Sometimes. Depends this term on whether we can get a new head-stockman and a new governess. John's out in the stock-camp, and Mary's filling-in in the schoolroom.

Q. Do you have a telephone?

A. Are you kidding? No, a transceiver.

The diary is a tougher proposition. It must be written up daily — no cheating and filling in a whole week in one hit like the station diary — and no romanticising because nothing very much has happened for days, and jazzing it up a bit for posterity.

Let's see:

Thursday: (a) Travel: Bore run 160 km. Old Harry in the ute. Left 7am. Pussycat Bore is only 16 km from town, so I may as well add another 32 km because Harry's hide's cracking, and sure as eggs he'll come back hours overdue claiming he got bogged for about four hours at the Overflow. Rations to the stock-camp. Me in the old truck, left 10am. Should have been 80 km, but they weren't where they said they'd be by today, and I had to track them up. Speedo not working, and across country — say 20 km, could be 25, took me four hours to find them, anyway. Said they thought it was Tuesday today.

(b) Visitors: 9am. Bunch of daffy tourists wanting petrol and directions. Took wrong track yesterday. Offered $50 note for petrol, but I had no change so I had to give it to them. Also mud-map. 5.30pm. Four Aborigines in old bomb, wanting petrol and tucker. Offered bag of dingo scalps in payment. Fair enough.

(c) Daily work program:

6am. Lit fire. Fed chooks, cooked breakfast, set bread.

7am. Housework. Explained correspondence lessons for Mary to teach little kids.

8am. Listened to traffic list on transceiver, collected two telegrams, sent one. Kneaded bread.

9am. Pumped petrol for tourists. Baked bread (six loaves for stockcamp). Knocked down remaining dough. Mary can bake that for us when the first lot's out .

9.30am. Smoko. Loaded stores for stock-camp.

10am. Bread out. Pumped petrol for old truck. Threatened little kids. Left for Bloodwood Yard to meet stock-camp. Ha-ha.

4pm. Home again. Clean-up, and cuppa.— Put roast on for tea. Kero fridge played up, needed new wick, so made one from leg of baby's flannelette pyjamas.

5pm. Charged transceiver battery, fed chooks, dogs. Mary watered garden, prepared vegies, bathed baby, and asked for rise in pocket money when she eventually gets back to school.

5.30pm. Pumped petrol for visitors, and served them from store. Pumped dieseline for lighting plant. Sod wouldn't start. Harry arrived — late, like I said — patronisingly took over, and the rotten thing started first go for him. (He can chop wood tomorrow. I know he hates that job!) I know he's been to town too, I can smell the beer on him. He couldn't admit he'd been in, could he, and bring me out some town bread. Not him. And I'll have to bake again tomorrow because I gave the Aborigines two of our four loaves. Well, after the wood he can clean down all the engines — he hates that worse than chopping wood. (Well, maybe not, or we might need a new handyman as well as a head-stockman.)

6.30pm. Tea. Sloppy ice-cream. Fridge smoking again. Fixed it while Harry told kids gruesome stories about kero fridges burning down homesteads from Boorooloola to Bourke.

7.30pm. Kids to bed. Bedtime story "Snow-white and the Wicked kero fridge" (dwarfs put out the fire, so hopefully kids won't have nightmares. That Harry!)

8pm. Galah session on transceiver, passed messages to neighbours to meet our stock-camp at Graveyard Gully on Saturday to take delivery of strangers. Heard next-door neighbour ask his head-stockman to keep an eye open on the road for the bag of dingo scalps he lost off the back of his truck this morning.

8.30pm. Mail day tomorrow. Wrote pleading advertisements head-stockman and governess, and lying letters to school principals re delayed returns of John and Mary.

9.15 pm. Started questionnaire and diary conscientiously.

9.35 pm. Dog tired. Printed brief lying letter with left hand to Survey chief saying right hand in sling so couldn't co-operate, very sorry. Chucked survey stuff in fire. Went to bed.

Social Workers in the Bush

Hey, ever been checked-out by a social-worker? If you live in the bush it depends on which paper you're reading as to whether you're an elitist capitalist pig, a hard-working member of the rural community, a farmer-equals-peasant, or don't exist at all. Whichever category you fit, the only common denominator is being non-urban, and that in some quarters is now being equated with "under-privileged".

I'd never given much thought to social workers because not too many ever pressed on regardless into the never-never. I knew they existed, the same as psychiatrists existed, but there didn't seem to be a crying demand for the services of either in the localities I frequented.

If you had financial problems you either got a job, borrowed from a mate, or poddy-dodged from an Overseas Company, according to your inclinations; if you had emotional problems you picked a rip-roaring fight, went on a bender, or eloped with somebody's spouse. The one thing you didn't do was whinge about your problems to somebody who wrote it all down in a little book, so it could be held against you later.

After all the epithets that have been tagged to country people over the decades, imagine my surprise to discover that "under-privileged" has now been added to the list to include whites as well as blacks. (Makes a nice change, doesn't it.)

Personally, I think there must be a Government glut of social workers, so they had to hunt around to find something to occupy them, and somebody decided there had to be possibilities in the word "remote". And the great thing about this idea was that the surfeit of social workers would not be so evident if the job involved a three-weeks journey into the interior instead of a three-hours jaunt poking into the least-savoury back-alleys of Kings Cross. So now it's the In thing to investigate the appalling problems which beset the dwellers in remote regions.

From what I can glean, there appears to be a sexist flavour to the operation — only women and children seem to be under-privileged at this point in time. Which is a pity, because the prospect of some young social worker, eyes alight with missionary zeal, telling a craggy-faced old death-adder that he's not living right, would be an event fraught with all sorts of interesting possibilities.

Let us consider our children through the eyes of the social worker. They are uinder-privileged because they don't have (a) peer-group companions, (b) primary school education, and (c) access to urban amenities.

Well, I'm not sure that peer-group companions are absolutely essential, because kids can pick up some awful things in a peer-group — like nits, disgusting table manners, drug-addiction, a profligate taste in music, and a vocabulary unintelligible to the remainder of the population.

Maybe there is a slight case for schools, but when you consider correspondence versus ordinary it soon becomes clear where the advantages lie. The correspondence pupil won't have to take a chance on whether he'll actually be taught to read and figure, or whether the teachers will be on strike or not. A parent can insist on a certain level of intelligence in a hired governess, but that's not an option in the school. Certainly you can be lucky, but consider the possibility of your child being subjected to the socialist teacher who is so rabid that he believes that you can nationalise brains (because that's his only chance of acquiring any.)

Maybe the bush child can't learn team sports, but I'll bet he's a lot fitter than the over-weight kids stuffing themselves on potato chips and cokes at school tuckshops throughout the country.

As for urban amenities such as art galleries, museums, libraries, swimming pools, and so on, there are many urban children who never get to see them, and many country children who do during their holidays. Moreover, the social workers don't seem to have considered the rural amenities at all. Urban kids can only dream of owning a pony or learning about nature first-hand. The kids are the best judges of what they need, and I've never heard a bush child yearning for an urban environment, or complaining of being bored, whereas the ability to entertain themselves seems to be a declining asset among the city youth.

The country kid has the best of both worlds.

Our bright-eyed and bushy-tailed young social worker would also strike fairly barren ground with the bush kids' mothers, because the environment shapes a different type of person to the one who really does need their services. Having been forced by circumstances to solve their own problems, a type of character evolves which resents what is seen as outside interference or just plain sticky-beaking. Unsolicited and inexperienced advice is taken as an insulting insinuation that you can't handle your own affairs, and merits and receives some fairly brusque replies.

If the situation does arise when you really need a hand, the friends and neighbours are always there, as you'll be when they are in trouble.

The women who live in remote places are generally too busy to be lonely, and have by necessity developed into the type who, if they considered they were under-privileged, would get up and do something about it themselves. The C.W.A. isn't an organisation which carts placards up the main street or expends its energy in vociferous abuse, but its list of achievements for the betterment of the lives of bush families goes far beyond what any social worker could dream up, and no drain on the tax-payer either.

So I doubt whether the social worker invasion is angled for success. In fact, the only one I know is an ex. She came, hesitated, re-assessed the situation in the light of on-the-spot observation, and then quickly snapped up a ringer. Now she's as happily under-privileged as the rest of us.

Seeding is for the birds
— mice, insects etc.

Sunday evening: Tomorrow the plane will arrive early to seed our frontage paddock with a mixture of buffel and rhodes grass, and a smaller area near the airstrip with a mixture of two buffels. All that in one day — makes you think, doesn't it. For thousands of years man used to sow his seed by walking up and down the furrows broadcasting it by hand. In some parts of the world they probably still do it that way today. It looks so pastoral and romantic in those old-fashioned water-colour paintings of golden-haired maidens in long gowns scattering the grain from a basket and singing as they work. I bet the grins would be wiped off their faces if they had to seed our frontage that way!

Monday evening: Modern technology — huh! The plane duly arrived, ingested bag after bag of mixed buffel and rhodes, and dutifully spread the seed over the ash-rich frontage. I sat in the shade of a tree beside the airstrip with a thermos and light lunch and photographed the various aspects of the operation — marvellous inventions, these agricultural planes.

Now for the smaller two-buffel strip. The seed merchant mixed some paspalum with this lot because the buffel seed is very light and there could be some slight difficulty in getting it to flow through the plane's seeding equipment. The plane takes off.

The pilot does the first run very quickly, so it must be okay. Or is it? He taxis up the strip and shouts from the cockpit, "Sorry, mate, no go! If you crawl underneath and hold the bags open we'll empty the seed back. Right! Sorry about that. Cheerio!"

Joe looked pretty forlorn sitting in the middle of the airstrip up to his neck in a heap of fluffy buffel seed, only some of which he'd managed to stuff back into the bags. I photographed him.

We discussed the problem over the evening meal. He said: "Well, if you start early and walk across the wind, throw out a handful say every six paces, you could probably do an acre in a couple of hours. You can carry enough to get across the strip and back, so you can refill on the road. Better start at the narrow end, because it's half a mile wide at the other end, and you'd better work up to that gradually. The secret is not to stop until you feel that you can barely make it back across the stretch to the road — crawling, that is!"

I stared at this monster who had promised to love and cherish me, but he continued unperturbed: "The sun will be pretty savage, so wear a big hat. Early night now, honey, so you can get a sun-up start."

Tuesday evening: I knew all along that he was only joking, but I thought I'd be on the safe side, so after breakfast I got out the sewing machine and started in on the split jeans and ripped shirts I've been promising to mend for months. I don't think it will come to mending the socks too, but I will if I have to.

It's been a day of experiments. Joe got an old washing machine from the dump and cut the bottom out and substituted chicken wire. Then he stuffed the washing machine full of buffel seed and hoisted it up on the end of the dozer's tree-pusher. As the dozer jolted along with the washing machine swinging from the tree-pusher some of the seed fell through, but every now and then the works got bunged up and Joe had to tug and jerk the rope he'd attached like a leading rein to the receptacle. I think there has to be a better way.

One week later: The job's finished. Joe did it the old-fashioned way. He broadcast it — only difference was he didn't walk up and down the furrows, he drove the dozer with one hand and scooped and hurled handfuls of seed from the bag on the seat beside him with the other. It took him the whole week and he had to keep at it without a spell because every day looked like rain. I didn't go near him with the camera; I stayed home and mended socks. Up and down he went, crunch, bash, crunching over logs and stumps, teetering into melon-holes, ducking sticks the dozer threw up, handling three levers and a bag of seed at the same time, with an extra big handful every time an errant whirly-wind veered in towards the dozer. It was a twenty-four hour a day job, because he was still flinging his arms around and vibrating and ducking in his sleep.

I finished the socks, washed all the curtains, and made a moderately successful sponge-cake, and I did make a small contribution to the seeding because the cat and I, between us, stood a twenty-four hour guard over the bags of seed in the shed which were the determined target of the mouse-plague we're having.

One month later: We certainly raced the storms all right — there's no sign of them yet! Who said we'd have an early Wet; we're probably not going to have one at all.

In the meantime we're having a grasshopper plague. There they go, millions upon millions of them, pirouetting through that seed dispersed with such blood, sweat and tears; tossing up clawfuls with gay abandon and catching it in their gaping maws; leaping, pouncing gleefully, and stuffing themselves till they bulge obscenely. The ants aren't half so ostentatious about their loot, and they're a lot more methodical too. They husk the seeds before they cart them underground. Every one of the millions of ant-holes in the buffel paddock has a ring of seed-husks around the entrance, and the busy little things are working overtime because the husk-mounds are growing in height and circumference before our eyes. Whenever an enterprising ant-scout finds a sizeable pile of seeds he whistles up a brigade to bore a hole down on the spot right through the middle of it — saves on transport, I suppose.

. . . It is my considered opinion that we ought to stick to range-fed cattle and forget all about this improved pasture. I suspect it might have been cheaper to have fed the seed direct to the cattle and saved the cost of the aeroplane and the wear and tear on Joe and the dozer. On the credit side, the socks got mended.

One moo doesn't make
a mob

My first close contact with a cow was at the age of nine with a small Jersey by the name of Peggy, whose warm teats at six o'clock on a dark frosty morning used to stir up the itchy chilblains on my fingers, so that milking her became a combination of frenzied squeezing punctuated by frequent pauses to lick the offending chilblains. I used to vaguely wonder why Peggy didn't get chilblains on her tits, considering how damnably cold that cow-shed used to get in winter-time.

Then I headed for warmer climes and the great fenceless expanses of the northern plains, where I discovered that the adjective "warmer" applied with a vengeance to the summer-time, but that winter temperatures could be as cold, if not decidedly colder, than the environs of Peggy's cow-shed. The only advantage was that the cold season didn't last so long.

The cattle there were Shorthorns, millions of `em, and any attempt to milk one was an exercise reserved for the annual rodeo, and involved a horse, a lasso, and a contestant with a foolhardy disregard for life and limb.

As far as I could see, the only reason they were called Shorthorns was because there was an even more dangerous breed called longhorns, which had a hornspan unchanged through generations of descent from the ancient aurochs, which had carried them specifically for stabbing into bailed-up sabre-toothed tigers.

As I pushed further into Deepest Australia I made contact, to a lesser extent, with another breed called baldy-faced, rather pretty red and white creatures, about which ringers sang mournfully at night as they rode a watch with the drovers' mobs. These, it seemed, were no more milkable than the shorthorns.

"Milk 'em?" replied a puzzled ringer to my inquiry. "You don't milk 'em; you eat 'em! You want milk, you get a coupla goats!"

The intrepid young journalist was learning daily what made the northern cattle industry tick. Most of it she learned from eavesdropping in outback bars, or round campfires, as owners and drovers of shorthorns and baldy-faces argued the relative merits of their mobs.

She gained the distinct impression that baldy-faces were comparatively recent infiltrators from NSW and Victoria, widely referred to as "Down Inside" and thereby suspect, because then, as now, some pretty funny ideas filtered through, which inevitably affected the well-being of God's Own North.

Baldy-faces were also more prone to pink-eye, swamp cancer, ticks and pleuro, and if you pushed the mickies around a bit they got sulky and chucked it in.

The Hereford owners claimed exactly the same list of deficiencies against the Shorthorns, but as they were in the minority, or couldn't shout as loud, the popularity of the Shorthorn prevailed.

Arriving at last in the farthest extremities of the great continent, in the fabled State of Queensland, the young reporter found yet a third breed — the yak — a new arrival from the north, a monstrous humped beast with long floppy ears and short smooth hair, with the speed of a horse, the kick of a camel, and a rodeo performance to outshine the gladiatorial combats of Ancient Rome.

Brisbane Show, on the fringes of "Down Inside" would not acknowledge the yak as representative of the cattle species, and refused the first contingent entry to the showgrounds, so that their owners had to hire a shed some streets away, and extol the breed from there.

Old ideas die hard, but the Brahmans proved themselves in the north; drought-resistant, tick-resistant, no eye or cancer problems, they were genetically suited to the country. The diehards said the meat didn't have the flavour of the British breeds, but more and more were persuaded for one reason or another to introduce Brahman bulls to their cows.

The islands of pure British breeds diminished, as Brahman bulls leapt nimbly over ordinary fences and took runups for the higher ones. The only difference between those who bought Brahman bulls and those who didn't was that the buyers got their yak-blood infusion a bit quicker. Braford, Brangus, Droughtmasters, the hybrid best of both types, have been established breeds for years now, spreading gradually across the whole of northern Australia.

Now that the breeds have been legitimised in their own right some southerners have been sneaking across the border to inspect them, and even to cast a glance or two at the pure-bred Brahmans.

Those long legs mean they can gallop faster in the scrub, but they also mean they can reach higher branches for top-feed in a drought. The bulls play merry hell with the fences when they fight through them, but what's a fence or two when there's red-blooded bush entertainment to be had to compensate for the withdrawal of most of our worthwhile TV.

Milk? Well, yes, they produce plenty, you can see that by the size of the calves, but any dash of yak blood probably means they can kick sideways as well as forwards and backwards, so maybe best you get a coupla goats.

Dingoes? Well, the cows like to chase dingoes; they hand their calves over to a friend to mind, and go all out after the brutes; wild pigs too, just for the fun of it.

The main difference between moving a mob of Shorthorns and a mob of Brahmans is that with Shorthorns you put one man in the lead and the rest on the tail, but with the Brahmans you put the whole darn lot in the lead and keep your fingers crossed.

Brahmans are very intelligent and tame quickly if you hand-feed them. They will help themselves to a bale of hay from the back of your vehicle in the yard, and they know how to undo the strings. But if they see you oiling the bolts on the yard gates one day not a single beast will turn up for a feed the next day. They contribute to a large extent to the high standard of stockmanship in the north: if you can out-think a Brahman, then you're pretty good!

Things that go bump in the night

Oh what a night of excursions and alarums I've just had. Last night was just like any other night until we put the engine off and darkness enfolded the homestead in its slumberous embrace. Darkness, of course, is the signal for all sorts of creatures to roll over, rub their eyes, and throw back the bed-covers, but usually their nocturnal peregrinations don't concern me because I am indulging in well-earned and conscience-free repose.

Last night I was hovering on the brink between wakefulness and sleep when a scrabbling sound from the bathroom intruded on my consciousness. At one end of the shed we have two bedrooms and a bathroom with only partitions between, no ceiling, so it wasn't really possible to ignore the increasingly-insistent scrabbling. I got up, took the torch, and spot-lighted a large mopoke sitting on the side of the bath, obviously ill-at-ease in the unfamiliar environment. It immediately opened its beak so wide that it needed no stretch of the imagination to realise that it would take my arm off at the elbow if I tried to eject it by hand. So with torch in left hand and broom in right hand I attempted to persuade it to climb on the broom-handle. It misunderstood my motives, and kept clashing its gaping beak open and shut and executing little dance-steps on the rim of the bath. Finally I poked it in the brisket, and as it sprang a few inches off the bath I shoved the broom-handle beneath it and hey presto — mopoke on mobile broom-handle perch. I carried it swearing (bird, not me) into outer darkness, launched it, and retired to my interrupted rest.

I was almost asleep again when soft footsteps on the partition above my head indicated that Zip, the cat, was up and about. This was a fairly common procedure; Zip has been patrolling the partitions and rafters for years. But last night was the first time he, for no apparent reason, halted above the sleeping hump that was Melissa, considered the possibilities of retribution and the chances of a quick getaway in the dark, decided the odds were in his favour, and hurled himself deadweight from a great height fair into the middle of Melissa. In the ensuing uproar Zip watched snickering from a rafter. Little did he know that he was going to get his come-uppance, and not too much later either!

Bed again, and Melissa and I beginning to feel we were being got at, while Joe and Pete snored on undisturbed.

Now, not too many people make the acquaintance of one mad bat in a lifetime. How come I get two! And why last night of all nights! I think this one sleeps by day on top of my wardrobe, and normally, when the engine goes off, I'm hardly in bed before I hear the soft swish and flutter as it does circuits and spirals over my head in the limited area between wardrobe and louvred window. (On the low swoops I pull the sheet over my head because I have this phobia about bats getting tangled-up in my hair.) After a few minutes to-ing and fro-ing Bat then exits through the louvres, and probably returns just before daylight.

Last night it was cold, so I had the louvres closed. It had always been quite evident that this bat was not endowed with extraordinary intelligence, but I had no prior reason to suspect that it also suffered from defective radar until it hit the closed louvres above my head with a thunk that was just as traumatic to me as Zip's assault had been to Melissa.

Torch again, and there was Bat plastered against the louvre with all the chitter knocked out of him. I opened the louvres, poked him tentatively, and he fluttered a wing like a bit of old umbrella, upside-downed himself, and hung suspended from the louvre edge eighteen inches above my pillow, panting and glaring. This position not being conducive to my immediate sense of security, I poked him again until he took the hint and fluttered through the now-open louvres.

But some distorted desire for revenge must have motivated him, because I was hardly back in bed again before he darted back in through the louvres and executed fast and vicious manoeuvres above my head, urinating indiscriminately as he went. Being pee-ed on by a crazed bat is not something that the average person faces with equanimity. It was not as if it was accidental — that mad bat did it on purpose.

If this sort of thing happens in broad daylight you can probably cope with it, but in the watches of the night it tends to assume outlandish proportions, and I didn't need Pete's cat-trap on top of what had already occurred.

A couple of years ago Pete concocted a Heath-Robinson contraption designed to catch a marauding wild-cat which had on occasions paid nocturnal visits to Zip's food-bowl. It worked on the principle that if the noose didn't catch the victim one of the other gadgets would, but due to limited success it had long ago been jettisoned. At least I thought it had.

I didn't know that Pete had seen the wild-cat reconnoitring the night before, or that he had rigged his cat-trap last night with modifications which promised a better result. Neither did Zip. Pete was asleep at the other end of the shed in a bed almost directly under the rafter on which Zip had earlier sought sanctuary.

I was finally sound asleep when Zip, carried away by his earlier success, decided to repeat his Melissa act on Pete. The lad woke with a roar, and the cat leapt sideways into the loop, which snatched his leg and simultaneously triggered the crash of three milk cans. It was seconds out of the ring, and that lot woke Joe too.

Pete said at breakfast that in the dark he hadn't seen that it was his own cat, and Zip obviously didn't recognise him either, considering the deep scratches on Pete's forearms and the battered cat now lying sulking in a basket.

Law of averages, it should be a quiet night tonight!

Cop this lot!

I dreamed that it rained; I suppose it was stimulated by a race-memory deep in my subconscious. No-one needs to be reminded of what the breaking of the drought will mean to Australia's farmers and graziers. We are pre-occupied, obsessed, with the need for water. The eternal round of pumping and rationing water; of carting fodder to starving stock; of pulling bogged animals from clutching mud-holes; of shooting those too weak to survive; of burning carcases — that doesn't leave much time for the normal station maintenance, and you can't stop pumping to overhaul the over-worked engines anyway, because you can't afford to get behind with the already-rationed supply of water. If the bore forks or the engine gives up the ghost your stock has had it. You don't dare think of these possibilities.

So you take your mind off it with the little things — drought's side-effects at the homestead — and you console yourself with comparisons of "when it rains".

When it rains there won't be any ants visiting my sink. Do you think they smell the water like cattle do? The little fellows climb up the wall and come in the kitchen window all day, but the big meat-ants are night-drinkers. If I'm a bit late with the washing-up after tea I find them racing backwards and forwards on the sink in a frenzy. When it rains the bush-bees won't need to crawl up inside the tap on the rain-water tank for a drink. When I fill the kettle I strain the water through a square of mosquito net and the little, rescued, black bees crawl off thankfully. Pete, first day home on holidays, didn't notice them when he filled the kettle. We had bee-tea.

We boil all our water now; it's got a funny taste. The inlet to the tank is thoroughly screened, but my theory is that there's a dead bunyip in there — got washed in as a bunyip egg, hatched, grew, expanded, expired. It's bore water pumped into the tank so it can't be the alternative of dead cattle, feral pigs, or kangaroos, which flavour the supplies of people who depend on dams or waterholes.

Topping-up the dogs' and chooks' water-containers won't be a constant job when it rains. They drink more in the hot weather, but most of it goes to the birds and the bees. The parrots waste a lot by bathing as well as drinking, and slopping it over the side. They're impatient creatures, won't wait their turn at the bird-bath. The poor old dogs have to compete with the bees and ants which drown themselves in millions and cover the surface area with a floating black raft of corpses.

What a difference the rain will make to the gardens in the outback — I mean the gardens still in existence because of a bore-water supply. There can't be many people left who could hold out against the soulful pleading of a dozen horses ranged outside the gate, staring at the lawn and salivating. It saves you mowing, but sooner or later they'll move further afield. If your back verandah isn't screened you'll likely find an inquisitive horse staring through the kitchen window eyeing off the dough you're pounding for a batch of bread. Norah Twistleton left the dough rising on the kitchen table, back door open, and went for a short nap. Jody's pony — named Pony — entered, sampled, got its nostrils blocked up with dough, panicked, crashed around for an exit, and defecated in fright. At lunch Norah mentioned to Ted that she wished it would rain soon.

For those who own free-ranging chooks and a watered garden, the chooks will scratch hollows in the damp earth under the shrubs for their afternoon siestas. For those with locked-up chooks and no garden left the dogs will scratch the hollows for their afternoon siestas in the shade beside the house wall. No houses have actually fallen down yet.

When there's no more need to feed out hay there won't be little sharp pieces of hay-chaff in the washing machine, which lurk in pockets and cuffs until they swirl free and make a bee-line for the inside seams of my jeans and shirts. Mandy says if I finished-off the seams properly the chaff couldn't catch. She gets embarrassed when I scratch in front of visitors.

There won't be chaff in the bathroom, hay in the bedroom, on the chair-seats, in the verandah beds, and there won't be any hay-storms right through the house when a willy-nilly whips across the hay-stack, dances tantalisingly across the yards, pretends it's going to miss the house, and then zips back and spins into the kitchen. Chaff-custard for the chooks' tea again!

A chaff-storm is worse than a dust-storm, but not much. You absolutely have to clean-up after a chaff-storm, but you can learn to live with every-day drought dust. Until it rains there is no way you're going to beat the dust: you can wield the feather-duster until you're blue in the face and screeching like a demented rooster, but all you do is stir up the atmosphere — the dust is going to settle before you. I just ignore it, dusting only obvious flat surfaces and, on one occasion, the bald head of a sleeping visitor.

We only have chicken-feed duststorms compared to what northern South Australia and western Queensland can turn on, so I'm not complaining. (Three-feet high dust mounds jamming the back door shut so you have to climb out the window and shovel it away before you can open the door, and I'm not exaggerating either — ask anyone who lives on the Birdsville Track or along the Diamantina.)

When it does rain, burning the rubbish isn't going to be the trauma it was last week-end. As the garbage-man doesn't call out our way I dispose of the household rubbish in a 200 litre drum which I burn off regularly, because if I don't, the crows will investigate it and scatter plastic bags and bottle-tops for a six-foot radius. The drum was a quarter full; there wasn't a breath of wind. I set fire to the rubbish and, fire-conscious, stood and watched it, because the hay-stack was only fifty yards away.

A willy-nilly came from no-where, dipped into the drum and snatched at some half-burned paper. It paused and dropped them beside the drum, and I dived with a shriek of terror and stamped them out. Then I swiftly poured two buckets of water into the drum, while the willy-nilly circled the haystack to show me what it had had in mind. Last month a fire which began in a road-house rubbish dump burned for miles. I'd better dig a hole and bury the rubbish from now on until it rains.

And when it does — just think — I won't get bogged in bulldust as I go to read the rain gauge. It'll be lovely, lovely mud instead!

As others see us

Robbie Burns wrote a little poem about seeing ourselves as others see us, but that's a sure way to schizophrenia if you live in the scrub. I am reminded of the verb conjugation — "I have a good appetite, you eat too much; he has all four feet in the trough." So let's take some examples of the image of the station family from different aspects.

You first: You see yourselves as hard-working battlers trying to keep one jump ahead of the voracious middlemen, and an uninformed, unsympathetic Government. You're fairly conservative, but willing to experiment on a likely innovation. Above all, you are a good solid citizen with a broad knowledge of Australian and world affairs, and a true assessment of where primary Industries belong in the country's economy.

Neighbours: A variety of opinions here. Those in the same circumstances equate you with themselves, but the magnates of the Big Company runs and the city solicitor-type owners regard you warily, suspecting you of everything from branding their cleanskins to borrowing their stud bulls. Still, they often think their managers are selling their cleanskins or lending their stud bulls, or selling meat on the side — that's why they change them so often. Nasty suspicious types.

Bank managers: They see you as sets of figures. When the figures are black they know they have a slippery hold on you, and they visualise you as some wild animal to be speedily ensnared by an expensive investment requiring a big loan. If the figures are red, you become a recalcitrant wrong-doer, in need of lecturing, punishment by high interest and extra bank charges, or even banishment by foreclosure.

Prime ministers: The view is that you belong to a minority group, too small to have any electoral clout, so anything goes. If he's Labor, you don't count, and if he's Liberal, he knows that the worst you can do is vote informal, and the chances are you won't.

Treasurers: They see you as landholders with vast acres of laden money-trees growing profusely right up to the back-door, every one with half-a-dozen flat, sleek bullocks resting in its shade.

Conservationists: To a conservationist the image is one of Dad rapaciously bulldozing down stands of 200-year-old endangered forest giants, Mum gleefully beating a wombat over the head with a shovel, and the kids getting little chain-saws in their Christmas stockings.

Animal Libbers: Lord knows what some of them think, or even how they think. But it's an even chance they picture you as the equivalent of medieval torturers, sadistically and systematically tormenting poor animals right up to the point where you sell them to a wicked henchman for filthy money.

Left-wing academics: Nasty brutes, these, with slitty eyes and little wispy beards, also infected with the medieval concept syndrome. (The female ones have two little wispy beards, only they grow them in their armpits.) To them, you are cattle barons, achieving huge estates, Cessnas and Mercedes by stamping on Aborigines, and exploiting the poor working men, the poor unemployed, the poor gays, the poor unmarried mothers, the poor drug addicts, and the poor you-name-its.

Aborigines: The ones who live in the scrub and work for you sometimes, think you are just mugs. Proper stupid to work your guts out and worry your head off seven days a week, year in and year out. More better you siddown quiet fella and wait longa that cheque Gubmint bin give; you gonna live longer that way.

Stock agents: They tend to see you as a shadowy figure in the fore-ground of clearly defined mobs of round-rumped bullocks, just right for the sale in a fortnight's time. Their merchandise blokes have their noses closer to the ground, sniffing out empty shelves in your shed, spotting noxious weeds on your roadside, and assessing what new products they might be able to talk you into purchasing. You can tell what the stock agents think of you by the number of the firm's notebooks they hand out, one in a dry year, but maybe six in a real-good year. (It's when you can't get one at all that you have to worry.)

City-dwellers: There are two images here. The upwardly mobile young, when at home in Australia, have an image of a straw-chewing yokel leaning on a fence and brushing away flies. However, once they get overseas the picture changes to a wide-hatted, check-shirted, elastic-side booted, free-striding Mel Gibson type, with whom they instantly identify by donning a broad-brimmed hat and a plaited belt with a knife pouch and singing "Click go the Shears" on street corners.

Show visitors: Patrons of capital city Royal Shows surely can't be blamed for seeing you as a privileged elite, owners of fine horses, stud stock, and flash cars. As astute exhibitors, you ought to consider an accompanying video film showing the run-up to getting your stock ready for the show. The best city comparison I can make is the well-groomed couple at the dinner party. What went before the grand appearance, like the row over how much Mum spent on the dress, and pinching the milk money to pay the baby-sitter, has its country equivalent, as you well know, but the show patrons don't have any inkling. Pity!

So there you are — a jolly mixture of Frankenstein, Dr Jekyll, Mr Hyde, Caliban, John Wayne, Simon Legree, Al Capone, Duke of Bedford, Mr Nice and the Village Idiot. So it's lucky you're all too busy keeping up the maintenance on your places to worry about your images. Otherwise, you might precipitate a rash of identity crises, thereby giving rise to a completely new industry of Scrub Shrink Clinics, and a line of Compudose Tranquillisers for the boss tossed in with the licks and the fencing pliers on the back seat of the agent's car.

Satire to let off steam

Mostly Downs,
December 1, 1988

Dear Sis,

We are still hoping that you and Pete can make it home for Christmas, but the situation doesn't look too promising at the moment, permit-wise. Mum managed to get a permit to travel to town through the Aboriginal Reserve, so she could take part in the Bi-Centenary celebrations, but somehow the Aboriginal Reserves director heard what she'd been up to — she dressed up as a pioneer wife in the procession — and now they won't give her a return permit to come back home. She drove as far as the Twistleton's place, and Ted would have flown her home in his plane, except that since the Government passed the Aboriginal Air-space Bill the reserve mob are really missile-happy.

We've had branding problems again this year. Dad got the permit for the vet to come, and the vet got the permit to travel through the Aboriginal Reserve, but the Animal Protection crowd took out an injunction against the vet because someone claimed he's once ear-marked a calf with a pocket-knife, and, as you know, the accused is now guilty until he's proven innocent.

So the vet is awaiting trial, and as far as the Animal Census people know, our calves aren't yet branded. Ha Ha!

Our latest court case doesn't come up until January. You know what the first storms of the Wet are like. Well, the lightning one night last week was terrific, struck a big tree and dropped it across the fence and laid a whole panel flat.

A couple of cleanskins went through the fence onto the road, and one was hit by some Greenie yahoos speeding in a Conservation Department vehicle: killed the beast, and made a nice mess of the front of the vehicle, so they have charged us because it happened on our frontage.

But we think we might win this one. Sam had the fence mended and the tree chopped up on the woodheap before dawn, and without saying so outright we've inferred that the cleanskins must have wandered down the road from the Aboriginal Reserve. The cattle there are all cleanskins, so it will sound plausible.

Dad says it will be no more that poetic justice, because that was the very tree the Conservation Department refused us a permit to lop last year.

Grandpa is still on a bond. When he went to town last month Dad asked him to bring back someone for a couple of weeks' casual work in the workshop, and he went to the CES and asked for a handyman.

They got him under the Sexist Act, and charged him the same day. He was so narked about it that he forgot to find a handyperson to bring home anyway, and now has to do the jobs himself.

But back to our current problem. I don't think you'll get an Aboriginal Reserve permit since Mum blotted the family copybook by indicating tacit approval of pioneers, but Norah Twistleton told us on the galah session that the Pig Power People are planning a rally in town the week before Christmas, and then a march through here to the Wildlife Reserve, where they will camp for Christmas.

They'll be passing through all the stations on the way gathering information for the projected Feral Farmers Act, and already have a group permit for the reserve. Perhaps you could join them, drop off when you get here, and we'll worry about getting you out again when the time comes.

It means a 150 km walk for you, but as they are all townies from Sydney and Melbourne they'll be stringing out like drought-stricken poddies after the first 50 km, and unless we can think of something better, Mum will sneak into the mob at the Twistleton boundary.

Oh, by the way, you'll be interested to know that we have a new resident on the station. He's Bill Blank, a landscape artist and sculptor, and Dad gave him permission to park his rustic old caravan down by the creek while he went on a historical painting spree. Nice chap — interested in getting down on canvas what the country looks like before the FF Act comes in.

He hadn't been there a week before a National Heritage Inspector arrived, and declared that the old broken-down yards the artist was painting, and the old caravan he was living in, be included in the National Heritage Register, which means they can't be removed or changed in any way.

Bill thought at first that he could get compensation to buy another van, but not so. In fact, under the new National Heritage Act, he has to caretake it at his own expense, maintain it in exactly the same condition. So, officially, he can't leave here.

At first he was livid, but when Dad showed him the flood level of the creek about 200 metres higher than where the van is parked he calmed down, and shifted all his gear out of it up to the house. When the first flash flood takes the van he'll be able to claim the insurance and leave the station.

In the meantime he is painting scenes around the homestead, and Dad has bought a painting of the house for Mum for Christmas, if she gets home. If not, for Mothers' Day.

The Dingo Land Rights Officer is due tomorrow, so I'll ask him to post this letter, as the mail delivery is doubtful this week. Last week the mailman's dog bit a greenie on the footpath in town, so the mailman has to go to court on an assault charge.

He expects to get off as the Pig Power People have taken up his case on the grounds of Animals' Rights to Retaliate; seems the greenie kicked the dog first. However, the case won't be heard till Thursday, which doesn't leave much time for this week's mail-run.

Dad was very pleased to hear that you both did so well in your law-course exams. He thinks it was an excellent idea for Pete to change over from his vet course, as vets are now considered little better than Feral Farmers, and a lot of them will be out of a dollar if the Pigs get their latest Act passed that any human castrating any animal be operated on in like manner.

Cheers. Hope to see you soon.

Love, Vanessa

P.S. The Chetwynd's last governess was a vegetarian. Chet put a bucket of oats and a bucket of water in front of her at the tea table. She didn't think it was funny and gave notice. So now Eunice says Chet has to find a new governess or teach the kids himself. V.

Epilogue

Slipping on a new harness

Sadly, I'm on my own now and, like a suprisingly large number of older women on bush properties, I have had to face the last big challenge. When the worst thing that can ever happen to you has happened and you've lost your mate, you have to put aside despair and carry on. Straight away, no breathing space. Maybe that's what saves you; you can't indulge your misery and work out the intricacies of the complicated water pipelines at one and the same time. In fact, as you stare at the multiplicity of pipes and stopcocks down at the bore, the main emotion is one of self-accusation.

"I ought to have known all this! Why wasn't I interested enough to ask?"

A long-indulged attitude becomes instantly reversed. The water supply to the house is NOT the most important. The tanks and troughs out in the paddocks are!

That is only the first reversal of outlook for the woman whose previous priorities centred on the home, feeding the troops, supervising the children's correspondence lessons and tending the garden. The metamorphosis is complete when you notice, 12 months down the track, that, on the bedroom dressing table, once again your hairbrushes share space with a pocket-knife, a small screwdriver and a handful of .22 bullets. And this time they are YOURS.

On a family property, particularly an isolated one, it is not gender-discrimination but just circumstances which have decrred that the wife and mother has spent most of her time, not out on the run learning the ropes, but tied to the homestead. You can't cart a young baby on a motor-bike to do a fence run; you can't supervise school lessons out in the stock-camp. You're at the homestead almost full-time so naturally you're elected cook and that job alone doesn't leave much time when you're feeding two or three hungry ringers as well as your own family. About the only hands-on contribution to what's going on in the workshop or the cattle yards is the hand on the telephone ordering a spare part for the dozer or telling lies to the stock agent you owe money to.

Years of this sort of existence lead to a complacency which, even when the children are no longer dependent, means that you generally stay in the same old groove. There's never been a demand for your input into the actual work and the day-to-day decision-making of cattle-husbandry. And, lets face it, you don't have the practical knowledge and experience to make a considered decision equal to your partner's. If you've ever given orders to the men, it's only been to pass on his instructions in his short absence. Anyway, if you're pushing sixty and pear-shaped, the prospect of a scrub-country muster on a nippy horse or a day's stint on the dozer doesn't have the same appeal it might have done when you were twenty. Taking smoko down to the stockyards and ordering the cattle-trucks for the sale are more in your line. You're an onlooker.

Then suddenly you aren't, you're it! Panic! "I can't! I know I can't!" But you can. There's an inner voice telling you that the cattle are doing a perish so you'd better get that pump engine started. No, fill the diesel tank first, you fool!

By the time your children who have been overseas have arrived back you have, with the help of your wonderful neighbours and, yes, the sympathetic agents too, got to the stage where you can reply firmly to the telephone enquiries about a possible sale of the property. Especially the one from the only neighbour you don't get along with.

"Are you thinking of selling?"

"No!"

"Bit hard to run the place on your own, isn't it?"

"Not at all! I'm thinking of turning it into a lion park. Can I count on your for half of the cost of the new boundary fence?"

It's not altogether true that the older you are the slower you are to learn new things. In some circumstances the learning process is almost instantaneous. You're isolated because of a flood; the generator engine is bunging on an act. There you are, on hands and knees, with the workshop manual spread open on the end of the cement block and a jam tin ready to hold the nuts and screws. You've swotted up that manual at a speed that would gladden the heart of any engineering instructor and the elation when you get the engine going again, just before the meat in the deep-freeze thaws right out, is heady stuff. By the end of the week you have permanently swapped your tea-towel for a grease-rag and you have all six engines on the place pinned down and a notebook filled-in with dates denoting the times to change their oil filters and air-cleaners and what brands of oil they drink. So you remember their particular idiosyncrasies you give them names. Any names will do but I favour politicians'. Tim sings along sweetly enough; Rob's reliable; Cheryl breaks down regularly for any reason or none at all.

The next hurdle is employing staff. Contractors for mustering and fencing are no problem; you can get recommendations from your neighbours if you don't already have regulars. But you know you can't do the day-to-day jobs your partner did so now you need a permanent station-hand.

There is no doubt that it is harder for a woman on a property to give orders to a male employee than it is for a man. Older male employees tend to question a female's decisions as a matter of principle; you have to be darn sure you're right before you give an order. So what to do to get them onside? Personally, I don't hold with the new-age feminism that sneers at using the old-style female wiles to get what you want. You know you can't dig postholes and keep up with the lads and, what's more, you don't fancy digging postholes; you've got better things to do. If it means that you have to flatter the big strong males and kow-tow to their egos to get the job done, then I say Go for it! All you have to be firm about is where you want the postholes to go, how deep, and how long they take to do it.

Strangely enough, the worker who wouldn't turn a hair if a male boss checked on the depth of a posthole resents it from a female. That's where you combine your snooping trip with taking him for smoko and having yours with him; works every time. Of course, I don't know how far you can go with the "flatter and feed" technique if you're only thirty years old and a potential candidate for a Miss Australia quest. Fighting off the advances of a lusting station-hand who thinks you've been encouraging him is not a problem for me, so it's up to the younger girls to work out their own solutions there.

After a certain period of time you will notice that the previous habits of a lifetime have subtly changed. There's no tea and bickies brought to your morning bedside and the fire's not alight. You light it yourself and, what's more, you split the kindling yourself. The woodheap's getting low and the cattle work's in full swing so the chances are you're going to take the chain-saw and saw up some logs on the flat yourself because the menfolk can't be in two places at once. (Only females can do that.)

You favour solid boots over dainty sandals and you don't have to shave your legs any more because you wear long pants all the time. You don't grumble now as you pick the grass-seeds out of the sox before they go in the washing machine; you're just thankful there's enough grass out there to seed. No more natty straw hats; your wide-brimmed Akubra has developed a distinctive shape and its very own oil-patches and grease-spots.

You've gradually extended your everyday vocabulary too to include things like gripples, and gripple-fasteners, and male and female threads and bastard files, and you can say the word "pizzle" instead of "thingo" to the vet without flinching.

You mostly go to town now in the Hilux instead of the car, and you don't whinge about cleaning the dust and lumps of mud and fencing pliers and multigrips out of the cabin and affixing the rego sticker that's been in the glove-box for the last six weeks. You remove the roll of fencing wire and the stray lengths of barb off the back, sweep off the layers of hay and dirt and the missing